PRAISE FOR

COMBING THROUGH THE WHITE HOUSE

"Theodore Pappas has written an erudite, witty, eminently charming book on a subject with surprising richness and depth. This is cultural history at its most entertaining, by turns moving and salacious. As Pappas ably demonstrates, a person's hair—especially when that person happens to be the most powerful man in the free world—is the product of so much more than a comb and a cut."

—SUDIP BOSE, EDITOR OF *THE AMERICAN SCHOLAR*

"Theodore Pappas's book does two things brilliantly. First, you'll learn surprising facts that will keep you busy at cocktail parties for the next century or two. Second, you'll see the world through a clarifying new lens. Because hair is everywhere. Hair weaves (sorry) its way into everything from politics, religion, literature, and identity. You'll never look at history—or the protein filaments on the top of people's heads—the same way again."

—A.J. JACOBS, *NEW YORK TIMES* BESTSELLING AUTHOR OF *THE KNOW-IT-ALL* AND *THE YEAR OF LIVING BIBLICALLY*

"Entrepreneurs see things that others miss. They leverage the past for a better tomorrow—and with his entrepreneurial approach to history, Theodore Pappas will help you see our country clearer, like wiping hair away from your eyes."

—JASON FEIFER, EDITOR IN CHIEF OF *ENTREPRENEUR* MAGAZINE AND AUTHOR OF *BUILD FOR TOMORROW*

"With his novel perspective, engaging prose, and entertaining eye for detail, Theodore Pappas has combed through the White House and teased out moving, little-known tales about our 'heads of state,' First Families, and country at large. Documentary producers would be wise to take note."

—KAREN AND HOWARD BALDWIN, PRODUCERS OF THE ACADEMY AWARD-WINNING FILM *RAY*

COMBING

Through the

WHITE HOUSE

COMBING
Through the
WHITE HOUSE

HAIR *and* ITS
SHOCKING IMPACT
on the POLITICS,
PRIVATE LIVES, *and*
LEGACIES *of the*
PRESIDENTS

THEODORE PAPPAS

Published by Harper Celebrate, an imprint of HarperCollins Focus LLC.

Note: Much of the content of this book is a result of the author's lifetime of work, including books read beginning in childhood, conversations, handwritten notes and journals, and personal experiences. The author has done his best to include sources where possible. If you find one of the stories particularly interesting or curious, the author and publisher invite you to explore the subject more closely for yourself.

Original illustrations: Heather Gatley
Art direction: Jen Showalter Greenwalt
Cover design: Katie Jennings
Interior design: Mallory Collins

ISBN 978-1-4002-4615-1 (HC)
ISBN 978-1-4002-4614-4 (epub)
ISBN 978-1-4002-4617-5 (audiobook)

Printed in Malaysia

24 25 26 27 28 COS 5 4 3 2 1

For my children—
Oliver, Cecilia Jean, and Demetrius

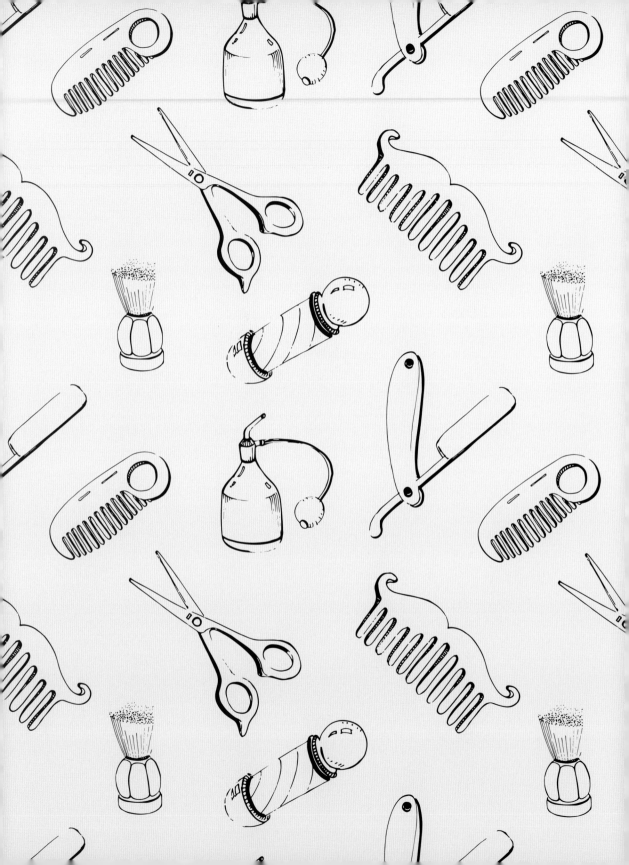

CONTENTS

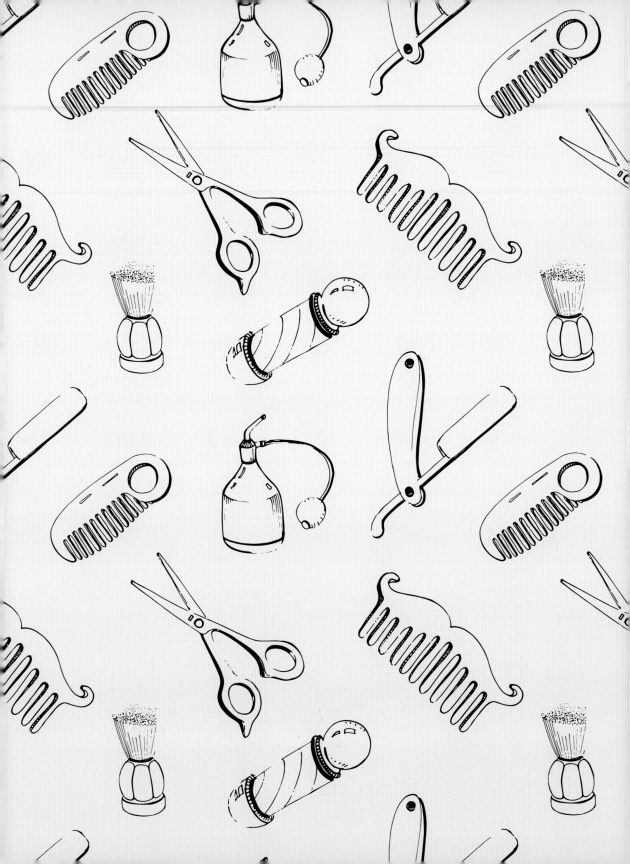

NOTE TO
THE READER

I've intentionally played fast and loose with symbols and synonyms for hair, using *follicles, filaments, tresses, strands, coifs, coiffures, locks, fur, mane,* and *plumes* interchangeably, fully aware of the terms' many differences. I did so out of respect for the reader's sanity should I not find a way, a fun and entertaining way, of diversifying the hundreds of references to our "plumage" that follow. I hope the reader will forgive this literary license.

INTRODUCTION

A NOVEL LOOK AT THE

Presidency

*T*here was nothing ostensibly special about the short meeting scheduled for the Oval Office on May 8, 2009. It was slated as a simple photo op. Carlton Philadelphia was leaving his post with the National Security Council, and he and his family were scheduled for a farewell photo with the president that departing staffers routinely receive.

After the photo was taken, Carlton's sons each wanted to ask the president a question. Barack Obama (44th US president, 2009–17) said fine. Eight-year-old Isaac asked a policy question, about why the president had cut funding for the F-22 fighter jet. "Because it costs too much," Obama explained. Isaac's five-year-old brother, Jacob, had a more personal question on his mind.

Hair Like Mine, photo by White House photographer Pete Souza, depicting five-year-old Jacob Philadelphia touching the hair of President Barack Obama, Oval Office, May 8, 2009.

"I want to know if my hair is just like yours," whispered the little boy, speaking so softly that Obama asked him to repeat himself.

Jacob did.

"Why don't you touch it and see for yourself?" encouraged the president. "Touch it, dude!"

Towering over the little boy, Obama bent over in front of the famed Resolute desk so Jacob could gently pat the president's head. White House photographer Pete Souza, at first caught off guard, recovered swiftly and snapped a quick shot for posterity.

"So, what do you think?" asked the president.

"Yes, it does feel the same," the little boy replied.[1]

For little Jacob, having hair like the president's proved something far deeper and more meaningful than a shared biological trait. As longtime Obama adviser David Axelrod later said, "Really what [Jacob] was saying was, 'Gee, you're just like me.' And it doesn't take a big leap to think that child could be thinking, 'Maybe I could be here someday.'" The photographer who took the iconic shot agreed. "I think a lot of young African American kids could identify with that moment," he said.[2] That moment, unscripted, and that photo, unplanned, live on as a "touching" reminder of the pride and hope that Obama's presidency generated in African Americans of all political stripes.

> *Having hair like the president's proved something far deeper and more meaningful than a shared biological trait.*

How exceptional, in the grand sweep of presidential history, was this hair-related incident in the Oval Office? In other words, could hair have been a factor, and a consequential one, in other presidential events, both remote and recent?

The shocking answer is yes.

Unbeknownst to many people, even many scholars, hair has played a

surprisingly significant role for centuries in the
"affairs of state." It has not only affected the personal and professional lives of the men and women
who have occupied the White House, influencing
how they discharged their public duties, but it has
even at times impacted the political landscape and
foreign policy of the country. These hair-tied tales
are little known and seldom discussed, but they
deserve wider notice, for they shine a meaningful
light on the evolution of the presidency and the events
and tragedies that have shaped the nation at large.
Moreover, given the ubiquity of hair as a feature of
life that everyone everywhere can relate to, such stories help personalize the past in a more intimate way,
offering us a novel manner of learning from history
that is refreshing, rewarding, and even moving.

Whether it's the madness of King George and his loss of the American
colonies, the murder and mourning of Abraham Lincoln, the secret "assassination" of Zachary Taylor, the sexual liaisons of Thomas Jefferson and John
F. Kennedy, the relentless body-shaming of First Lady Barbara Bush, or the
strange twists and turns of the 2020 election—hair can elucidate all these sub-
jects, and many more.

AT THE CENTER OF EVERYTHING

Hair's ability to "shed" these novel insights stems from one fundamental fact:
hair is seldom simply *hair*. Though hair is a basic feature of human life and
the larger vertebrate class of animals called mammals, providing warmth and
protection to sensitive and strategic areas of our bodies, the true significance
of our tresses is nearly always far greater than the sum of their biological parts.
Anthropologist Grant McCracken understood this some thirty years ago when

he wrote: "The study of hair, I found out, does not take you to the superficial edges of our society, the place where everything silly and insubstantial must dwell. It takes you, instead, to the center of things."[3]

Throughout history, at this "center of things," we find hair as a major cultural signifier, highly charged with meaning and unspoken messages. The messages are varied, shedding light on a host of social and cultural issues, from personality, gender, power, age, race, and social standing to conceptions of beauty and religious faith. In fact, as demonstrated by the incident with Obama in the Oval Office, hair not only "signals" but can even *inspire*.

Here's a sampling of hair's significance and various meanings over time:

- **Strength and devotion:** There are scores of references to hair in the Bible. Most famously, the long, lush locks of Samson the Nazirite, whose vow forbade the cutting of his hair, mirrored his strength and devotion to God. In return, the LORD later assures us that "the very hairs of your

  head are all numbered," reflecting His sweeping care and concern for us. During the anointing of Christ, Mary washed Jesus' feet with expensive oil and then wiped them clean not with a towel but with her tresses, foreshadowing the foot washing and same selfless act of humility that Christ would perform at the Last Supper.[4]

- **Rituals and rites:** From ancient Egypt and Phoenicia to Greece and early Rome, hair commonly delineated gender and social-class differences and was even

Samson and Delilah, engraving by Bible illustrator Gustave Doré, 1866.

sacrificed in rituals intended to curry favors from the gods—for fertility, safe passage, or strength in battle. In ancient Athens, when a young man reached the age of puberty, his hair was cut in a sacred ceremony, with the shorn strands dedicated to a deity. A similar tonsure rite of passage is common among Hindus and Buddhists, with the hair of babies commonly cut to mark a break with past lives and the child's purification.[5]

- **Dangerous and beguiling:** The seductive power of hair is a staple of Western literature, from the infamous snake-hair of Medusa, who turned her beholders into stone, to the long-haired, bodice-ripping hunks on the covers of paperback romance novels. Women with long, unbound hair are seen as especially beguiling in assorted religions, leading to mandates requiring them to cover their tresses in public (and even veil themselves) in deference to piety and sexual modesty. Christianity, Judaism, and Islam all have religious mandates or customs related to veils and head coverings for women, and in Sikhism, even the men are required to cover—with turbans—their long, uncut hair.

- **Status and servility:** The long and piled tresses of the affluent women of ancient Rome were often conditioned with dead leeches, urine, and pigeon excrement; dyed with earthworms, ashes, boiled walnut shells, and vinegar; and braided and curled into towering, crownlike designs. However, the female slaves who executed these intricate treatments and "ornate" updos—the *ornatrix*—were

Head of Medusa, pen, ink, and charcoal drawing by artist Godfried Maes, 1680.

forced to wear their hair short and simple as a sign of their servitude and diminished social status.[6]

- **Divine and magical:** Followers of Muhammad ecstatically collected his hair (and sweat, fingernails, and saliva) for the talismanic powers it supposedly possessed. The collected hair would be worn in the cap of a warrior desiring strength in battle or placed beneath the tongue of a deceased Muslim as an act of veneration. Consequently, Muhammad's hair was wildly coveted. When a single strand was stolen from an Indian mosque

in 1964, riots ensued, leading to deaths. Assorted indigenous cultures and African religions even perceive our locks as the locus of the soul, seeing strands of shorn hair as holding a special power, useful in love potions, good-luck charms, and medicinal cures, as well as demonic spells.[7]

- **Royalty and ruin:** Laden with symbolism were the heaven-touching hairstyles of France's Marie Antoinette. The queen's thinning hair was augmented to outrageous heights—sometimes more than a yard—with wiglets, pads, and hidden wire contraptions, reflecting the excesses and decadence of the French aristocracy. Radical democratizers during the French Revolution countered such excesses with the blade of the guillotine. The queen's executioner even cut her hair before her beheading; a similar shearing and dehumanization was reportedly done to Joan of Arc and Anne Boleyn before their executions.[8]

- **Nationalism and conformity:** In 2021 a Japanese student finally won her multiyear lawsuit after the "hair police" at her school banned her from

Young Muslim women wearing religious headwear during a protest against Denmark's ban of face veils, in Copenhagen, Denmark, August 1, 2018.

Le Negligé Galant Ornés de la Cœffure à la Belle Poule

Coiffure à la Belle-Poule, artist unknown, 1778. This painting depicts a ship atop a pouf—a decorative hairstyle with ornaments, jewels, and other items to share a theme or tell a story—worn by Marie Antoinette to celebrate the victory of the French frigate, *La Belle Poule*, over the British in 1778.

functions due to her refusal to continue dyeing her brown hair black, to conform with the black, straight hair of almost all other Japanese students; the years of school-mandated dyeing had caused rashes on her scalp.[9] A more vicious example of nationally mandated coif conformity occurred on the Caribbean island of Dominica, when the Dread Act of 1974 led to the arrest and even killing of citizens wearing dreadlocks, which were seen as symbols of rebellion and spurs to uncivilized behavior, such as smoking marijuana and practicing Rastafarianism in the largely Catholic country.[10]

- **Color and character:** In the early Roman Empire, women with blonde hair or bright yellow wigs were nearly always associated with prostitution. This association continued in medieval Britain, where prostitutes advertised

their availability by wearing bright yellow hoods. Thanks to the "blonde bombshell" effect, blondness continues to be tied to lasciviousness today. Redheads have similarly faced stereotypes, associated throughout history with treachery, deviance, and hotheadedness—and even witchcraft, lycanthropy, and vampirism. A "National Kick a Ginger Day" in Canada in 2008 attracted thousands of followers on Facebook, prompting police to investigate the organizer of the campaign for possible hate crime violations.[11]

- **Oppression and protest:** Whether long, short, or shorn, hair has been one of the most common and visible

Vietnam War protesters demonstrate at a "Get Out of Vietnam" rally at the San Francisco Civic Center, by photographer Bob Kreisel, circa 1969.

signs of political control, power, and protest. The examples are legion, from the short-haired flappers of the 1920s, long-haired hippies of the 1960s, and large Afros of Black activists of the 1970s to the shaved pates of "skinheads" and #MeToo activists.[12] But the most poignant example is the shaved head of the Holocaust victim. When the United States Holocaust Museum in Washington, DC, received a shipment of twenty pounds of human hair from the Memorial and Museum of Auschwitz-Birkenau, site of one of Nazi Germany's most notorious death camps, the donation set off an intense debate within the museum regarding whether to display these highly personal remnants of barbarity. The museum chose not to, displaying instead a mural of the shorn hair.[13]

Photograph of starved Jewish prisoners with shaved heads standing together at the Ebensee Concentration Camp after liberation by the US Army 80th Division, in Ebensee, Austria, May 7, 1945. Photographer unknown.

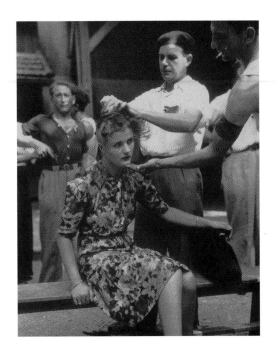

- **Rights and freedom:** Hair is commonly at the center of legal battles over an individual's rights. For example, is the length and style of a student's hair a constitutionally protected exercise of free speech? Are "induction haircuts," whereby the military shocks new recruits into their new environs, unfair and illegal when performed on a woman? Can police departments legally ban facial hair, when some 60 to 80 percent of African American males suffer from pseudofolliculitis barbae (PFB), a condition akin to "razor bumps" that can be embarrassing, painful, and permanently scarring, but which can be prevented by not shaving and hidden by beards? Could a fingerprint-laden coffee cup discarded by a suspect be fair game for seizure and police analysis, but not the hair or microscopic skin cells unconsciously left behind by the suspect? Does such "naturally shed DNA" trigger protections under the Fourth Amendment and an expectation of privacy? In step the courts![14]

HAIR, HISTORY, AND THE WHITE HOUSE

As shown in the above examples, hair can serve as a unique and useful lens for viewing and gleaning insights into any number of peoples, cultures, and social and historical events. It can also, by extension, serve as a novel way of

A woman in Montélimar, France, has her head shaved as punishment for her collaboration with German Nazis, August 29, 1944.

understanding certain institutions as well, and the events and personalities that have formed them over time—like the American presidency.

Hair, in fact, unearths a rich mine of surprises surrounding the US presidents and the White House.

Chapter One highlights Abraham Lincoln—the greatest US president to many—and recounts how he used his homely appearance, unkempt hair and all, to his political advantage, detailing the many unusual ways that hair (including facial hair) played a role in his life, public career, and even death—the first presidential assassination in American history.

Chapter Two shows how the once widespread tradition of collecting hair, an especially popular Victorian pastime, has served throughout history as a tangible and durable way of remembering our loved ones, honoring our leaders, and memorializing the US presidents, from George Washington and Abraham Lincoln through John F. Kennedy to the present day.

Chapter Three reveals the surprising way that issues and incidents involving hair have intersected with and influenced the personalities, private lives, and marriages of assorted presidents, occasionally even affecting the political landscape and foreign policy of the country.

Chapter Four traces the multifaceted ways that hair and image-making shaped the politics, public life, and private affairs of John F. Kennedy, even affecting how his family and the country memorialized the slain president.

Chapter Five relates the parallel tragedies of the Pierces and the Bushes and the unique role that hair played in how each family, exactly one hundred years apart, dealt with the heart-wrenching death of a child—tragedies that forever changed how the three presidents and the First Ladies performed their public duties.

Chapter Six then highlights how science, medicine, and technology—and hair analysis and DNA—have served as a forensic Sherlock Holmes of sorts, solving several long-lingering mysteries associated with the lives and legacies of assorted presidents and First Ladies.

A GALLERY *of* US PRESIDENTS

GEORGE
WASHINGTON

JOHN
ADAMS

ANDREW
JACKSON

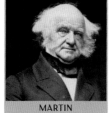

MARTIN
VAN BUREN

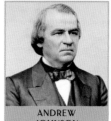

WILLIAM HENRY
HARRISON

JOHN
TYLER

JAMES
BUCHANAN

ABRAHAM
LINCOLN

ANDREW
JOHNSON

ULYSSES S.
GRANT

BENJAMIN
HARRISON

GROVER
CLEVELAND

WILLIAM
MCKINLEY

THEODORE
ROOSEVELT

HERBERT
HOOVER

FRANKLIN D.
ROOSEVELT

HARRY S.
TRUMAN

DWIGHT D.
EISENHOWER

JIMMY
CARTER

RONALD
REAGAN

GEORGE H. W.
BUSH

BILL
CLINTON

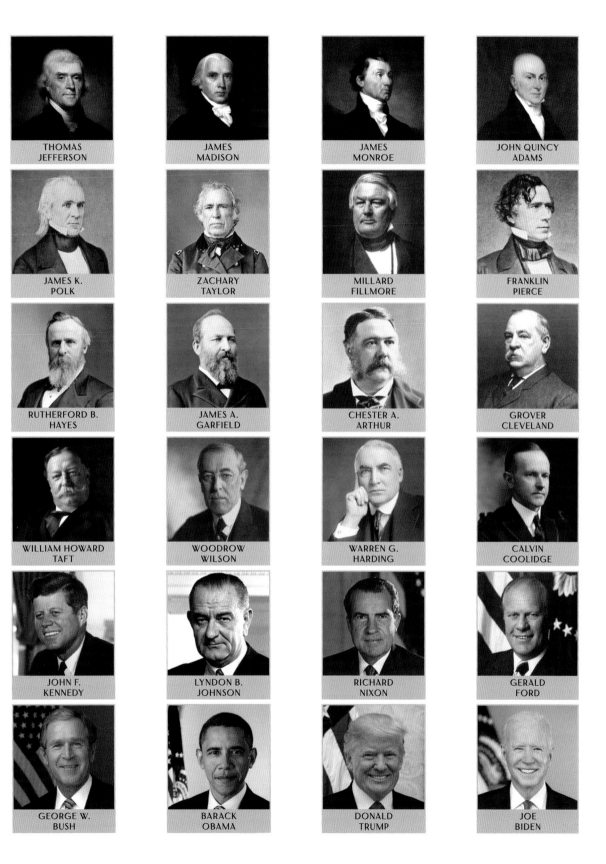

THOMAS JEFFERSON

JAMES MADISON

JAMES MONROE

JOHN QUINCY ADAMS

JAMES K. POLK

ZACHARY TAYLOR

MILLARD FILLMORE

FRANKLIN PIERCE

RUTHERFORD B. HAYES

JAMES A. GARFIELD

CHESTER A. ARTHUR

GROVER CLEVELAND

WILLIAM HOWARD TAFT

WOODROW WILSON

WARREN G. HARDING

CALVIN COOLIDGE

JOHN F. KENNEDY

LYNDON B. JOHNSON

RICHARD NIXON

GERALD FORD

GEORGE W. BUSH

BARACK OBAMA

DONALD TRUMP

JOE BIDEN

CHAPTER ONE

THE "BODY POLITIC" OF A PRESIDENT

HAIR AND THE LIFE AND DEATH OF

Abraham Lincoln

Hair masked the mark of the bullet that changed history. In fact, when twenty-three-year-old Charles A. Leale—an army doctor just six weeks out of medical school, in attendance at Ford's Theatre that fateful night on April 14, 1865—finally made his way through the frantic crowd and reached the president, the first doctor to do so, he didn't know for certain that the famed leader of the United States had been shot.[15]

After all, upon shooting President Abraham Lincoln (16th US president,

1861–65) at about 10:15 p.m.—a shot timed to coincide with a funny part of the ongoing play's third act, so that the audience's laughter would muffle the sound of the gun—John Wilkes Booth, the popular twenty-six-year-old actor and extreme Southern sympathizer, theatrically leapt from the presidential box to the stage below while brandishing not a firearm but a long silver knife, a dagger covered in blood. He reportedly waved the weapon while shouting, "*Sic semper tyrannis*" (the Latin motto of the state of Virginia, meaning "thus always to tyrants") and "the South is avenged!"

After shooting Lincoln, Booth had used the blade to attack Major Henry Rathbone, a guest sitting with the president and First Lady that evening. Given his proximity to the president, Henry had clearly heard the *CRACK!* of Booth's six-inch Derringer pistol, fired into the back of the president's head. The shot prompted Henry to rise to his feet and, through the thick and choking gun smoke that filled the presidential box, try to apprehend Booth and prevent his escape. But during the struggle that ensued, Henry suffered a ghastly wound; Booth had sliced him along the length of his left upper arm, nearly down to the bone, right through his biceps, if not also an artery. Henry began bleeding profusely, spewing blood on the dress, face, and hair of his theater companion: his fiancée and stepsister, Clara Harris (the daughter of Ira Harris, US senator from New York), the

Photograph of Abraham Lincoln before he grew his beard, by Alexander Hesler of Chicago, taken in Springfield, Illinois, on June 3, 1860.

fourth guest in the presidential box that evening. The metallic tang of warm blood stung the inside of Clara's mouth.

Horrifically, this would not be the last time that Clara's face, hair, and clothes would be covered in blood. Eighteen years later, on December 23, 1883, driven mad by guilt over his inability to save Lincoln from Booth's attack that tragic night, Henry would reenact the assassin's devilry, killing his beloved wife, Clara, by shooting her several times, then stabbing himself repeatedly in an attempted murder-suicide. After attacking Clara, Henry embraced his dying wife and kissed her hair, now drenched in blood for the second time in her life. He would spend the remainder of his days in an asylum, dying in 1911.[16]

Driven mad by guilt over his inability to save Lincoln from Booth's attack that tragic night, Henry would reenact the assassin's devilry.

"Oh, my husband's blood! My dear husband's blood!" cried the hysterical Mrs. Lincoln, mistaken but terrified upon seeing the blood-covered Clara. "Water! Water!" screamed a stunned and petrified Clara, finally realizing the nature of the red sticky substance now saturating her and wanting nothing more than to wash it off as quickly as possible. "I am bleeding to death,"

Slide depicting John Wilkes Booth leaning forward to shoot President Abraham Lincoln as he watches *Our American Cousin* at Ford's Theatre in Washington, DC, April 14, 1865. Unattributed, circa 1900.

muttered an increasingly weak (and increasingly forgotten) Henry. And all the while, amid the cries and commotion, copious blood, smoke, and uproar, with the actors and audience frenzied and bewildered as to what exactly had just happened, the president sat quietly, secretly bleeding in his chair from a wound hidden and hindered by one singular attribute—his thick black hair.

BODY-SHAMING A FUTURE PRESIDENT

Hair might now be masking the wound that in hours would kill the president, but a few years earlier, hair had contributed to Lincoln's safety and even aided his political career. In fact, Lincoln's overall appearance, locks and all, had played a significant role his entire life—from his humble days as a poverty-dogged boy on the Kentucky prairie, born in a one-room, dirt-floor log cabin, to his death in Washington fifty-six years later.

Hair might now be masking the wound that in hours would kill the president, but a few years earlier, hair had contributed to Lincoln's safety and even aided his political career.

As a child, the gaunt and gangly Abe was an especially easy target of ridicule, the kind of pitiful prey whom cyberbullies and body-shamers devour on social media today. Girls teased the tousled-haired giant without mercy, calling him as "thin as a beanpole" and as "ugly as a scarecrow." Others compared him to a dressed-up skeleton, and an oafish one at that, given his fondness for a single suspender to keep his pants from falling.

As an adult, a more arresting individual could hardly have been found, not least because of Lincoln's unusual height. Not only was the president impressively tall, but he was *unnervingly* so. At a time when the average height of an adult male was about five feet six inches, Lincoln towered at seven feet when wearing his beloved stovepipe hat. Furthermore, his ears, arms, hands, and feet appeared strangely oversized, giving rise to speculation among historians in the next century about whether Lincoln suffered from a genetic disorder called Marfan syndrome.[17]

Moreover, his sad-sack appearance (his "melancholy," folks called it) was more depressing than inspiring, and the tortured landscape of his leathery, asymmetrical face—so mapped and measured during his presidency by a new technological marvel of political force, photography—featured sallow, sunken cheeks, with a mole, no less; a ruddy, crooked nose; an inflated lower lip; a drooping eyelid; and cavernous eyes amid dark lines and crevices that conveyed, *in toto*, more strain and struggle than success and strength.

Media of the day were merciless in their mockery of Lincoln and his looks. The *Charleston Mercury* proclaimed him a "horrid-looking wretch,"[18] while a Houston newspaper branded him "the leanest, lankiest, most ungainly mass of legs, arms, and hatchet face ever strung upon a single frame."[19] Nor did Lincoln's own secretary of war, Edwin Stanton, pull any punches when it came to his boss's appearance, calling him a "damned long-armed ape,"[20] which was not an uncommon comparison among media pundits and political cartoonists once the hirsute Lincoln became America's first bearded president. In fact, Lincoln's hairiness and supposed simian-like features became a metaphorical constant in the rich torrent of vitriol issued daily against him. That Lincoln was widely ridiculed, even hated, in his time—by not only opposition Democrats but also members of his own Republican Party—is startling to many people today, given the polished lens of reverence through which the president is overwhelmingly now viewed. But Lincoln was deified in the tomb by the very folks who had detested him in the flesh. The racial tightrope of moderation and conciliation that Lincoln tiptoed, balancing principle with the necessary burden of pragmatism, infuriated many and satisfied few at the time.

> *Lincoln's hairiness and supposed simian-like features became a metaphorical constant in the rich torrent of vitriol issued daily against him.*

Even the hallowed Gettysburg Address, though lavishly praised by

Republicans and now ranked among the greatest orations in history, was excoriated in its day—yes, by Lincoln's political opponents, but by others too. "Anything more dull and commonplace it wouldn't be easy to produce," reported the London *Times* about the two-minute, ten-line masterpiece of 272 words.[21]

But it was the president's appearance—his body and physical features, and his perceived pilosity and apelike qualities in particular—that his critics often showcased. Mark Bowden, in a 2013 article in *The Atlantic* tellingly titled, "'Idiot,' 'Yahoo,' 'Original Gorilla': How Lincoln Was Dissed in His Day," recounts how nasty (and possibly dangerous) these verbal attacks on the president became:

George Templeton Strong, a prominent New York lawyer and diarist, wrote that Lincoln was "a barbarian, Scythian, yahoo, or gorilla." Henry Ward Beecher, the

Abraham Lincoln depicted as tightrope walker Charles Blondin, *Harper's Weekly*, September 1, 1864.

Connecticut-born preacher and abolitionist, often ridiculed Lincoln in his newspaper, *The Independent* (New York), rebuking him for his lack of refinement and calling him "an unshapely man." Other Northern newspapers openly called for his assassination long before John Wilkes Booth pulled the trigger. He was called a coward, "an idiot," and "the original gorilla" by none other than the commanding general of his armies, George McClellan.[22]

Of course, not everyone endorsed or engaged in this rhetorical war on the president. Poet Walt Whitman, for example, who adored Lincoln while acknowledging the very strange figure he cut, found shades of beauty lurking behind the bizarre. Lincoln's face was "so awful ugly," he suggested, "it becomes beautiful, with its strange mouth, its deep cut, crisscross lines, and its doughnut complexion."[23]

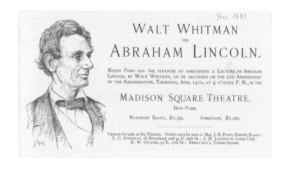

Lincoln's manner of dress only added to his ungainliness. As historian Richard Current suggested, if clothes make the man, they *unmade* this man, which is seldom an asset for a politician. Writer Nathaniel Hawthorne noted Lincoln's "ragged slippers" and "rusty black frock coat and pantaloons," in addition to the president's unkempt locks. "His hair was black, still unmixed with gray, stiff, somewhat bushy, and had apparently been acquainted with neither brush nor comb."[24]

Lincoln's manner of dress only added to his ungainliness.

English journalist Edward Dicey noticed a similar tatteredness, remarking on how Lincoln's suit was "unfashionably tight, creased in the wrong places, and also soiled" and that his "pants were too short and the gloves too long—too long even for his bony fingers."

A public announcement for a lecture by Walt Whitman on President Abraham Lincoln, to be held at Madison Square Theatre in New York on April 14, 1887.

Nor could Dicey ignore the president's noggin and untamed hair, for it was "a head, coconut shaped and somewhat too small for such a stature, covered with a rough, uncombed and uncombable lank dark hair, that stands out in every direction at once."[25]

From head to toe, from hair to boots, Lincoln was the cynosure of every eye and the object of endless scrutiny and editorial spleen.

Even when Lincoln's special qualities were finally gleaned, the revelation was hardly instantaneous. He was still too imposing, too gawky, too utterly odd for any swift waning of the very strange shadow he cast. Like the photoreceptors of our eyes that need time to transition from darkness to light, some period of adjustment was needed to first scan and take in the totality of this idiosyncrasy of a man. But according to Harold Holzer, this interlude was brief:

He was still too imposing, too gawky, too utterly odd for any swift waning of the very strange shadow he cast.

> They all [firsthand accounts] seem to say, for the first ten minutes I couldn't believe the way he looked, the way he sounded, his accent. But after ten minutes, the flash of the eyes, the ease of his presentation overcame all doubts, and I was enraptured. . . . I am paraphrasing, but there is ten minutes of saying, what the heck is that, and then all of a sudden it's the ideas that supersede whatever flaws there are.[26]

Now, Lincoln freely acknowledged the liability of his looks. He was fond of telling a story about an ugly man on a horse who had politely pulled to the side to let a lady rider pass.

> She stopped in turn, and said, "Well, for land's sake, you are the homeliest man I ever saw." "Yes, madam, but I can't help it." "No, I suppose not," she said, "but you might stay home."[27]

Full-length portrait of Abraham Lincoln, 1860.

Few doubted that Lincoln himself was the "ugly man on a horse" who had suffered the insult.

When Illinois senator Stephen Douglas, during one of his debates with Lincoln, accused the future president of being two-faced, Lincoln memorably quipped, "Honestly, if I were two-faced, would I be showing you this one?" On yet another occasion, when he learned that his always-testy secretary of war had progressed from calling him an ape to a fool and a baboon, Lincoln took the news with faux astonishment. Other leaders might have sacked a subaltern guilty of such insolence, or at least reproached him, but not Lincoln. What bothered him, said the president, was not Stanton's comments but that Stanton had a penchant for being right.

And it was exactly in this manner—with his self-deprecating humor and humility, along with his calm, compassion, charm, sincerity, decisiveness, and eloquence—that Lincoln countered the deck so obviously stacked against him, rose above the unflattering figure he cut, and warmed audiences large and small, both political and personal, to his favor. "He knew that he was ugly, ungainly, awkward in society," noted the great polymath and pedagogue Jacques Barzun, but "he did not resent these deficiencies [and] neither tried to cover them up nor referred to them continually from embarrassment. They were part of him . . . as a fact of nature."[28] In other words, Lincoln had learned early on to accept himself as he was, startling stature, mannerisms, looks, and all, and from this acceptance he gained strength, confidence, and even leverage over others who might otherwise have turned his deficiencies against him.

Lincoln had learned early on to accept himself as he was, startling stature, mannerisms, looks, and all, and from this acceptance he gained strength, confidence, and even leverage over others who might otherwise have turned his deficiencies against him.

Lincoln's masterful use of his "body politic"—this shrewd ability to transform the "liability" of his looks into a personal and political asset—was wonderfully depicted in the opening scene of the acclaimed film *Lincoln* (2012). During a conversation with a Black soldier upset about racial inequality, Sir Daniel Day-Lewis, in his Academy Award–winning role as Lincoln, listens politely, says he understands the issues, and then asks the young man what he'll do after the war. When the soldier says he could never be a barber because he can't cut hair, the president sympathizes and shifts the spotlight to his own insufficiencies, just like the real Lincoln did throughout his life. "I've yet to find a man could cut mine so it'd make any difference," he jokes. "My last barber hanged himself. And the one before that. Left me his scissors in his will."[29]

With his self-deprecating crack and reference to something as universal and relatable as hair, the president succeeded, if only for a moment, in bridging that always-treacherous chasm of race, building in the process some goodwill and trust that would be essential in the future, should the races ever peacefully coexist.

THE FAMED FACIAL HAIR

Despite the shrewd way that Lincoln could turn his supposed personal shortcomings to his benefit, he was still open to suggestions for improving his homely appearance. And what many folks suggested as a solution to Lincoln's "problem" was *hair*—in particular, *facial hair.*

As Republicans in New York remarked, Lincoln "would be much improved in appearance, provided [he] would cultivate whiskers, and wear standing collars." In Westfield, New York, an eleven-year-old supporter named Grace Bedell agreed, and it was her letter to Lincoln in 1860 that finally convinced the future president to grow his now-famous

What many folks suggested as a solution to Lincoln's "problem" was hair—in particular, facial hair.

Hon. Abraham Lincoln, Republican candidate for the presidency, 1860, lithograph by Leopold Grozelier, et al., showing Lincoln before he grew his iconic beard, 1860.

beard. As she wrote to Lincoln in Springfield, Illinois, on October 15:

I am a little girl only eleven years old, but want you should be President of the United States very much so I hope you wont think me very bold to write to such a great man as you are. Have you any little girls about as large as I am if so give them my love and tell her to write to me if you cannot answer this letter. I have got 4 brother's [sic] and part of them will vote for you any way and if you will let your whiskers grow I will try and get the rest of them to vote for you[;] you would look a great deal better for your face is so thin. All the ladies like whiskers and they would tease their husband's [sic] to vote for you and then you would be President. My father is a going to vote for you and if I was a man I would vote for you to but I will try and get every one to vote for you that I can.

It was her letter to Lincoln in 1860 that finally convinced the future president to grow his now-famous beard.

Lincoln appreciated the letter and suggestion, but he wondered whether growing a beard would spur as many gibes as votes, since all presidents before him (except for John Quincy Adams and Martin Van Buren and their cheek-snaking side-whiskers) had been clean-shaven.

Lincoln replied to Grace on October 19:

My dear little Miss.

Your very agreeable letter of the 15th is received. I regret the necessity of saying I have no daughters. I have three sons—one seventeen, one nine, and one seven, years of age. They, with their mother, constitute my whole family. As to the whiskers, having never worn any, do you not think people would call it a silly affectation if I were to begin it now?

Your very sincere well wisher

A. Lincoln

Despite his misgivings, Lincoln heeded the little girl's advice and took the plunge, growing the famed facial hair that completed *the look* now indelibly planted in world memory.[30]

Although the beard, as Lincoln had feared, spurred many a dig, such as the simian-linked wisecracks mentioned above, his new facial hair did indeed improve his appearance in the eyes of many, granting him an air of dignity, a new respectability, and some needed definition against the landscape of American politics. "A vigorous growth of comely whiskers has entirely changed his facial appearance," reported a correspondent from Springfield, and "the improvement is remarkable. The gaunt, hollow cheeks, and long, lank jawbone are so enveloped as to give fullness and rotundity to the entire face."[31]

Growing the beard, it seems, was a politically prudent move. But one man in particular abhorred the new whiskers, as writer Sara Kettler has noted. "In 1860, Milton Bradley had produced a lithograph of a beardless Lincoln. But Lincoln's new facial hair rendered Bradley's inventory out-of-date and useless." With his celebrity print business in a shambles—

Growing the beard, it seems, was a politically prudent move.

Bradley had made *hundreds of thousands* of copies of the cheek-smooth Lincoln portrait—the printer pivoted to a new product, one that would make him world-famous in the century to come. "Without Lincoln's beard," suggests Kettler, the lithographer's new career—and his pioneering game company, Milton Bradley—"might not have happened."[32]

Photograph of Abraham Lincoln, by Alexander Gardner, taken on November 15, 1863, just a few days before his famed Gettysburg Address.

Clean, Hairy, Clean: Facial Hair and the Presidents

That, in a nutshell, with few exceptions, is the three-phase history of presidential facial hair.

For the first half century in American history, presidents were typically clean-shaven, like our wigless but powder-haired first president, George Washington. In fact, a clean, whisker-free look was common in the eighteenth century among the educated class, which included the Founding Fathers. They were cultured and learned men of wealth and status, distrustful of democracy, protective of the vote, and suspicious of dirty populism and scruffy mob rule; they were denizens of the cosmopolitan East Coast, where trade and business flourished, and the Ivy League colleges and first libraries took root. Facial hair was fine for the frontier trapper and poor, country farmer, but it was beneath the dignity of the polite, self-respecting gentleman.

True, there were some hairy exceptions to this clean-shaven period in White House history—especially after the Founders died, their children gained power, and the country pushed farther into the rough-and-tumble frontier beyond the Appalachian Mountains. But these exceptions were subtle, falling short of complete beards and mustaches, as demonstrated by the bushy side-whiskers of John Quincy Adams (6th US president, 1825–29) and Martin Van Buren (8th US president, 1837–41). "Sideburns" (albeit large ones) are what we'd call such facial hair today, though this label is historically inaccurate in this case, since the word "sideburn" is a later creation, a play on the surname of Civil War general Ambrose Burnside, whose fame stemmed less from success on the battlefield than from the weird, woolly worm of side-whiskers and mustache that traversed his face. Large side-whiskers of this sort are also popularly called "muttonchops" (because they resemble the narrow end and broadening surface of a chop of meat), but this term, too, is a later creation, first used in this context in 1865. To the linguistic purist, then, "side-whiskers" were possible before Burnside and the Civil War, but not "sideburns" or "muttonchops."

The full beard of Abraham Lincoln (16th US president, 1861–65), the first president born west of the Appalachian Mountains, marked a sea change in presidential grooming. Save for two exceptions (Andrew Johnson, 17th US president, 1865–69; and William McKinley, 25th US president, 1897–1901), the hairy phase in White House grooming sparked by Lincoln lasted for another half century, from the beard-gruff fighting men of the Civil War era to the curly mustachioed tenure of William Howard Taft (27th US president, 1909–13).

Taking a razor to this hairy phase was the Progressive Era (1890–1920) and its spate of public-health reforms, all rising in response to the country's rapid industrialization and urbanization. To control the spread of disease,

reformers called for shorter hemlines for women, so their dresses, skirts, and bustles would no longer drag along the dirty, germ-laden streets, as they had throughout the nineteenth century; bans on spitting and laws requiring spittoons in public spaces; and clean-shaven men, so infectious diseases like tuberculosis could not hide and fester in their beards. The result, in the words of *Harper's Weekly* in 1903, was a "revolt against the whisker,"[33] spurring a cleaner, sleeker new look for the new male on the move at the dawn of a new century on the verge of the auto age. This clean "new look" has dominated presidential politics ever since. Except for some brief holiday stubble—as when President Harry Truman (33rd US president, 1945–53) grew a light goatee and mustache while vacationing in Key West after the hard-fought election of 1948—every president since Taft left office in 1913 has been clean-shaven.

The 1948 election, in fact, was a key moment in grooming history. Republican Thomas Dewey, the three-time governor of New York, was predicted in every major poll to defeat the Democratic incumbent, President Truman. So confident were folks of Dewey's pending triumph that the *Chicago Daily Tribune*, in one of the most embarrassing missteps in newspaper history, released an early edition of the paper emblazoned with a banner headline that read, "Dewey Defeats Truman." Two days after his upset victory, an ecstatic Truman gladly held up the notoriously wrong paper and smiled broadly for the cameras. His joy was palpable in the resulting photograph, which ranks among the most famous in American political history.[34]

But how had Dewey defied the odds, snatching defeat from the jaws of certain victory and delivering a gut punch to the polling profession still felt today? How had he blown it? Most historians have pointed to Dewey's aloofness and pomposity, as well as . . . *his mustache*, which he had grown for his girlfriend (who became his wife) in the 1920s. In the opinion of many, his Clark Gable–like facial hair was an affectation at odds with the

Harry S. Truman holding the *Chicago Daily Tribune* with the erroneous headline "Dewey Defeats Truman," at Union Station in St. Louis, Missouri, after winning the 1948 US presidential election. He was so widely expected to lose that the *Tribune* boldly went to press with a headline that assumed victory for his opponent, Thomas E. Dewey. Photograph by Byron H. Rollins, November 4, 1948.

clean-shaven seriousness and soberness needed in a modern president. As explained in 1944 by political columnist Helen Essary, who was nonetheless impressed with Dewey's intelligence and command of the issues, his mustache "takes from the seriousness and strength of his face. . . . You see only the mustache. You remember only the mustache. Without it, Governor Dewey would look a million percent more real as the proper man for the White House job he is after."[35] Especially damning for Dewey was the observation of Alice Roosevelt Longworth, Theodore Roosevelt's eldest daughter, famous for her biting wit. The well-dressed, mustachioed Dewey, she said, looked not like a president but like the dapper little bridegroom atop a wedding cake. It was a stinging rebuke, one that shadowed him for life.

This prejudice against presidential facial hair continues to cast its shadow today. After former vice president Al Gore lost the agonizing presidential election of 2000 to George W. Bush (43rd US president, 2001–09), the demoralized Democratic candidate disappeared from the limelight—and grew a beard. To TV talking head Chris Matthews, the newly bewhiskered Gore looked "like a Bolshevik labor organizer."[36] More significantly, in the eyes of political commentators of the day, the hairy change in Gore signaled one important thing: his retreat from presidential politics. He was done.

Hair, once again, is seldom simply *hair*.

From Political Improvement to Personal Safety

If Lincoln's beard contributed to his political career, it likely contributed to his personal safety as well, during the lame-duck period between his election to the presidency on November 6, 1860, and his inauguration on March 4, 1861. This was a particularly dangerous time for the president-elect, a period filled with as many well-wishes from admirers as death threats from haters—especially from Southern slave owners.

Of special concern was Lincoln's safety while traveling by train on the twelve-day journey from Springfield, Illinois, to Washington, DC, for the

The First Reading of the Emancipation Proclamation before the Cabinet, painted by Francis B. Carpenter at the White House in 1864, engraved by A. H. Ritchie circa 1866.

presidential inauguration. In fact, by the start of his journey on February 11, seven slave-holding Southern states had already seceded from the Union, a new country—the Confederate States of America—had already been declared three days earlier, and the fateful firing of shots on Fort Sumter by Confederate forces that would finally spark the Civil War was only eight weeks away.

This was a particularly dangerous time for the president-elect, a period filled with as many well-wishes from admirers as death threats from haters.

The vast majority of some seventy towns that Lincoln would pass through on his journey to the capital posed little threat. For example, Lincoln's train stopped briefly in Westfield, New York, where, embedded in the crowd thronged at the station to meet the president-elect, was little Grace, the girl responsible for his now-famous beard. As she later recorded,

> [Lincoln] climbed down and sat down with me on the edge of the station platform. "Gracie," he said, "look at my whiskers. I have been growing them for you." Then he kissed me. I never saw him again.[37]

But not all cities would be as welcoming as Westfield. Especially in Baltimore, Maryland, slaveholders seethed with anger at the soon-to-be president.

Compromising Lincoln's security were the newspapers of the day, which trumpeted the detailed timetable for Lincoln's train journey. As writer Daniel Stashower has noted, "From the moment the train departed Springfield, anyone wishing to cause harm would be able to track his movements in unprecedented detail, even, at some points, down to the minute. All the while, moreover, Lincoln continued to receive daily threats of death by bullet, knife, poisoned ink—and, in one instance, spider-filled dumpling."[38]

Lincoln downplayed the danger, much to the frustration of his advisers and assistants. "His mail was infested with brutal and vulgar menace, and warnings of all sorts came to him from zealous or nervous friends," wrote John Nicolay, one of his private secretaries. "But [Lincoln] had himself so sane a mind, and a heart so kindly, even to his enemies, that it was hard for him to believe in political hatred so deadly as to lead to murder."[39]

> *"But [Lincoln] had himself so sane a mind, and a heart so kindly, even to his enemies, that it was hard for him to believe in political hatred so deadly as to lead to murder."*

Lincoln's nonchalance is shocking to readers today, so accustomed are we to seeing the Secret Service (which didn't begin operations until three months *after* the killing of Lincoln, and then mainly to battle the counterfeiting of currency, widespread at the time) smother the US president always and everywhere. But this unconcern for presidential safety was common then. After all, the United States was then nearly a century old, and there had been only one attempted assassination of a president, back in 1835, on President Andrew Jackson (7th US president, 1829–37); the assassin's guns misfired, saving the president's life, whereupon the aging Jackson beat his attacker with his cane.

Assassination was just "not an American practice or habit," reassured Secretary of State William Seward.[40] In fact, this was the excuse given by Washington police officer John Parker for why he reportedly abandoned his post (there are conflicting accounts of his actions that night) guarding the entrance to the president's box at Ford's Theatre on the night of the assassination—he apparently left first to get a better view of the stage and performance, and then exited the theater entirely with the coachman and footman of Lincoln's carriage, to drink at the saloon next door. "I did wrong, I admit, and have bitterly repented," he said. "I did not believe anyone would try to kill so good a man in such a public place, and the belief made me careless."[41]

Lincoln's view of his personal safety was tied to his larger vision of government. In fact, he equated public access to the president with American democracy. "It is important that the people know I come among them without fear," he wrote. "It would never do for a President to have guards with drawn sabers at his door, as if he were, or were assuming to be an emperor," he told John Hay, another of the president's private secretaries. Lincoln took great pride in this shockingly open, open-door policy. He even encouraged strangers to visit him at the White House, and they did, strolling in off the street, lining the halls of the Executive Mansion, sitting on the floors, all with the hope of cornering the president and bending his ear with a special plea or request for this or that. Lincoln didn't mind, and if he had the time, he gladly listened. "I call these receptions my 'public opinion baths,'" he said, "for I have little time to read the papers and gather public opinion that way; and though they may not be pleasant in all particulars, the effect, as a whole, is renovating and invigorating."[42]

Lincoln considered proximity to the people he led to be essential not only to American democracy but to sage leadership as well—so critical, in fact, that

Abraham Lincoln's Last Reception, lithograph by artist Anton Hohenstein, 1865.

he had no qualms about firing officers under his command for breaching this critical rule of conduct. Lincoln's presence at Ford's Theatre on the night of the assassination was tied directly to his headstrong belief in a leader's obligation to the people he represented. The president really didn't want to go to the theater that evening, but he felt it *his duty* to attend. As he told his bodyguard, "It has been advertised that we will be there [at Ford's], and I cannot disappoint the people."[43]

Lincoln's frequent indifference to his personal safety nonetheless terrified others. "The President is so accessible that any villain can feign business," noted Hay, "and, while talking with him, draw a razor and cut his throat."

Lincoln's frequent indifference to his personal safety nonetheless terrified others.

Two others who were especially concerned about the president's safety were Samuel Morse Felton, president of the Philadelphia, Wilmington and Baltimore Railroad, and Allan Pinkerton of the Pinkerton National Detective Agency, one of whose clients was the Illinois Central Railroad. Both men understood the president-elect's vulnerability to harm, if not assassination, during his long train journey to Washington for the inauguration, and, in fact, they uncovered rather quickly a plan to kill Lincoln that subsequently became known as the Baltimore Plot.

Although historians disagree on various details of the plot and the level of danger it posed, it was still perceived as a serious threat at the time, leading Pinkerton to unleash a host of countermeasures, especially in and around Baltimore. He cut telegraph lines to hinder communication between cities, hired undercover agents, infiltrated secessionist circles, spread disinformation, arranged for decoy train cars, and hustled Lincoln on an earlier train that entered Baltimore in the middle of the night, ahead of the announced schedule. He even convinced Lincoln to pose as the "invalid brother" of a young traveler (Kate Warne, America's first female detective), to don a disguise—a

Portrait of Abraham Lincoln, oil on canvas, by artist George Peter Alexander Healy, 1869.

ridiculous looking low-cut soft cap, which Lincoln could pull down over his face, and a high-collar shawl—and to stoop and limp as he entered the passenger car of the train carrying him to Maryland, so that he appeared shorter than his striking six-foot-four-inch frame.

Also helping the covert plan was Lincoln's new look. Although many Illinoisans had seen Lincoln's newly grown whiskers, there were no Twitter-type means or cable-news services for keeping the country quickly abreast of such quotidian news as a politician's latest style of personal grooming. As Brad Meltzer notes in *The Lincoln Conspiracy*, "Outside of Illinois, [Lincoln] is still largely unknown. Relatively few Americans have laid eyes on him, and few Governors or Mayors have ever met him."[44] Even citizens accustomed to pictures of the president-elect likely had a prebeard image of him that was out-of-date.

As mentioned earlier in the case of Milton Bradley, hundreds of thousands of lithographs of Lincoln still circulating from the time of his election continued to present him as clean-shaven. In fact, as Harold Holzer has noted, during the president elect's train journey eastward to his inauguration, "he [Lincoln] sported such a bushy beard that crowds welcoming him occasionally failed to recognize him."[45] In other words, much to Lincoln's favor, not all denizens of Baltimore were on the lookout for a *bearded* president-to-be.

Such precautions and subterfuge—in conjunction with Lincoln's new appearance—worked to perfection, and the president-elect arrived safely in Washington on February 23, much to the chagrin of Baltimore's would-be assassins, including the reputed leader of the plot, the Corsica-born immigrant Cypriano Ferrandini. (Ironically, when the chevron-mustachioed Ferrandini wasn't busy plotting an attack on the president, he was single-mindedly focused on an altogether different subject: hair. He was the longtime barber at Baltimore's fashionable Barnum's Hotel, the very hotel where, in 1864, John Wilkes Booth would gather with *his* coconspirators to plot *their own* assault on the president.)

Surprisingly, instead of hearing praise for his wise security measures, the president-elect was ridiculed in the press, mocked by cartoonists for his supposed "cowardice." Lincoln had feared this would happen. "What would the nation think of its President," he had wondered, "stealing into the Capital like a thief in the night?"[46] Lincoln was furious and embarrassed in equal measure, and never again, he vowed, would he conduct himself in a way that undercut the public perception of courage and honor he wanted always to convey. Lincoln's subsequent fondness for little personal security throughout his presidency has been traced by many to this very episode in his preinaugural life.

THE HAIRY DETAILS OF LINCOLN'S DEATH

Hearing the cries from the balcony upon Booth's attack on Lincoln, Dr. Leale fought his way to the president's box, where he found Lincoln slumped slightly to the side in a high-backed, red-silk rocking chair. The president was unresponsive, barely breathing, with his eyes closed and his chin on his chest.

A frantic Mrs. Lincoln propped up her dying husband and pleaded for the doctor's help. Leale pushed the president's head upright and confirmed that Lincoln was alive, but there was no obvious wound that the doctor could inspect. The president, in fact, had the look of someone who had simply dozed off. He obviously needed to be examined, so with the help of two men who had also now entered the president's box, they laid Lincoln on the floor, whereupon Leale suddenly felt a bit of blood beneath the president's left shoulder.

The president, in fact, had the look of someone who had simply dozed off.

Supposing that to be the area of the stab wound, Leale ordered one of the men to cut off part of the president's clothes from that section to facilitate an examination. Leale then ran his fingers through the president's thick black hair (which Lincoln dubbed his "mane"), and there, finally, behind Lincoln's left ear, he discovered the gunshot wound in the back of Lincoln's head. There was, in his words, "a large firm clot of blood which was firmly matted with the hair." After removing the clot, "[I] passed the little finger of my left hand directly through the perfectly smooth opening made by the ball. . . . When I removed my finger which I used as a probe, an oozing of blood followed and he soon commenced to show signs of improvement."[47]

Although this lessening of the intracranial pressure helped the president to breathe more easily, his pulse remained weak. Other doctors then arrived on the scene, helping Leale to massage the president's chest, raise and lower his arms, and perhaps breathe air into his mouth (there are conflicting accounts of this), but the president remained unconscious, in dire condition.

Everyone agreed that the president needed to be moved, if only to prevent him from dying on a filthy theater floor. But move him to where? Returning the seriously wounded president to his own bed at the White House via a slow and bumpy carriage ride was out of the question; he would die in transit. So, amid the pandemonium in the theater and now outside as well—with

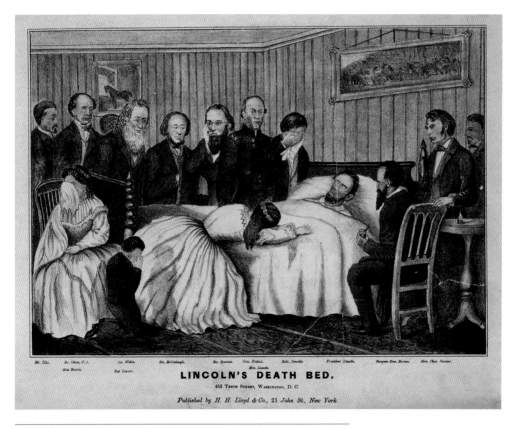

LINCOLN'S DEATH BED.
453 TENTH STREET, WASHINGTON, D. C.

Published by H. H. Lloyd & Co., 21 John St., New York.

Lincoln's Death Bed, colored lithograph, published by H. H. Lloyd & Co., 1865.

bystanders shouting, "Is he dead? Is he dead?"—a group of doctors and volunteers gingerly lifted the bloody and now bare-chested president and carried him down the narrow stairs of the theater, proceeding outside and across the street to a boardinghouse owned by a German tailor, William Petersen, and his wife, Anna.

One of the several doctors who helped move the president was Charles Taft. "The motion of the body in being carried," he noted, was a messy, delicate affair, "and my hands, which supported [Lincoln's head], were covered with blood and brain tissue." In fact, the procession across the street had to stop every few feet, so that Leale could reinsert his finger through Lincoln's hair and into his skull to unclog the hairy clotting that was causing pressure on the brain and further distress for the president.[48]

Slowly they pushed on, finally navigating the tricky curved stairs adorning the entrance of the Petersen House. They carried the president to a back bedroom on the main floor, where they found Lincoln's height too large to fit lengthwise on the bed. They tried to break off the footrail of the bed to make room for the president, but it wouldn't budge. So they positioned Lincoln diagonally across the mattress, propping up his bleeding head with two large pillows; his size-fourteen feet dangled off the end. In an eerie twist of fate, Booth had reportedly slept in the same bed just weeks earlier while visiting a friend in Washington.

Chaos reigned inside and out of the Petersen House. Secretary of War Edwin Stanton quickly took charge, establishing a communications center in an adjoining room, checking on the location of Vice President Andrew Johnson (soon to be sworn in as the next US president) and monitoring the status of Secretary of State William Seward, who had been stabbed repeatedly in his bed by a second conspirator at the same time that Booth had attacked the president.

Nearly forgotten amid the bedlam was Major Henry Rathbone, whom Booth had seriously wounded with his knife. While soldiers and physicians were running about, locating candles and situating the president in the back room, Henry grew pale from loss of blood and lost consciousness in the

While soldiers and physicians were running about, locating candles and situating the president in the back room, Henry grew pale from loss of blood and lost consciousness in the hallway.

hallway; a narrow slab of pale flesh sliced open to the bone peeked through his ripped sleeve, soaked with blood. Although still in shock from the attack and soaked in blood herself, Clara Harris admirably gathered her emotions and applied a much-needed tourniquet to her fiancé's arm, saving his life.

While Dr. Leale undressed the president and found blankets to cover him, Dr. Taft passed his finger through the president's hair and into the head wound as Leale had previously done and declared the bullet too deep to touch. A small amount of brandy and water was then applied to the president's lips to spur a response and some movement.

Lincoln's personal physician, Robert King Stone, soon arrived on the scene, joining a rapidly growing crowd of doctors, family members, friends, political leaders, cabinet members, and concerned citizens tramping through the hallway and streaming in and out of the house and the president's room—in all, some fourteen doctors and sixty others (perhaps as many as ninety) would visit the president's bedside during the final hours of his life. In fact, later depictions of the death scene in text and art placed so many dignitaries

Portrait of Robert King Stone, the physician who served President Abraham Lincoln, and who was present at his deathbed and autopsy, source unknown, circa 1860s.

alongside the dying president that the narrow section of the boardinghouse where Lincoln lay has been dubbed the "Rubber Room" for its endless elasticity.[49]

Dr. Stone proceeded with his own examination of the wound. What he noticed first was that the president's hair and scalp had hardly been affected and were not burnt at all by the lead ball fired into Lincoln's head at close range; as Dr. Leale had discovered, the wound was perfectly round and easily accessible. Stone then attempted to find and remove the bullet. He parted the president's hair and, as Dr. Leale had done right after the shooting, and Dr. Taft did as well at the Petersen House, probed the half-inch wound with his unwashed finger—he was now the *third* doctor to insert his unsanitized finger into the president's skull.[50]

He was now the third doctor to insert his unsanitized finger into the president's skull.

This maneuver is shocking to the modern reader, but before the invention of X-rays and the wide acceptance of the germ theory of disease, this was a common medical practice, done without an anesthetic, though it often caused more harm than good by introducing bacteria into the wound. This is exactly what happened to President James Garfield after he was shot at the Baltimore & Potomac Railroad Station in Washington, DC, on July 2, 1881. A dozen doctors probed and prodded the wounded president so aggressively (all with unsterilized fingers and instruments) that they grossly expanded a three-inch wound into a twenty-inch, pus-infected gorge, leading to his painful death eighty days after the shooting and his tragic status as the second US president to be assassinated.[51]

In Lincoln's case, as his autopsy would describe it, the pistol ball had traveled "obliquely forward toward the right eye, crossing the brain and lodging behind that eye. In the track of the wound were found fragments of bone which had been driven forward by the ball which was embedded in the anterior lobe of the left hemisphere of the brain."[52] Once again, the constant clearing of the bullet's pathway of blood, hair, and brain matter enabled the president to breathe easier, at least for a spell.

A small silver probe was then inserted into the wound, tracking the

Once again, the constant clearing of the bullet's pathway of blood, hair, and brain matter enabled the president to breathe easier, at least for a spell.

straight and neat course of the lead ball—hitting hard substances, likely skull fragments, along the way—but the projectile remained stubbornly hidden. An even longer instrument (a Nélaton probe) was then used, and though some of the doctors believed they had finally felt the deep-set ball, the projectile remained impossible to extract, whereupon further explorations of the wound (other than keeping it open and free from coagula) were abandoned.

Clearly, there was nothing more to do except wait—wait for death—and make the president as comfortable as possible. Mustard poultices and jugs of hot water were lined along his body, underscoring the vast chasm that existed between the primitive medical practices of the day and the advanced killing capacity of modern weaponry so horrifically on display during the Civil War. Stating the obvious, "all such aid was useless in a wound of this character," noted Dr. Stone in his report, written on paper stained with the president's blood.

There, in this cramped and crowded room, the morbid vigil proceeded throughout the night and into the morning of April 15. Visitors stood and sat around the president's bed, amid the blood-speckled sheets and freshly soaked pillows, some in hushed silence, others murmuring prayers. Doctors checked the president's breathing and heartbeat regularly, religiously recording rates in their notebooks. Others openly wept and shook their heads in sorrow and disbelief.

Everyone watched with a quiet intensity as the president's respiration lifted his bedsheet with each breath, and when the doctor pulled down the sheet to check his heartbeat, observers were amazed at the president's strong physique, so frequently masked by his loose, ill-fitting suits. "His brawny chest and immensely muscular arms revealed the hero of many a successful wrestling-match in his youthful days at New Salem," noted Assistant Secretary of the Treasury Maunsell Field. The wounded leader's "vital power was prodigious."[53]

Even with death on the doorstep, Lincoln's appearance remained a matter of deep scrutiny and commentary.

The bullet, which had come to rest behind Lincoln's right eye, caused the pupil to dilate wildly, and soon the eye was blackened considerably. "The least touch of his body surface," noted Stone, "would cause an electric jerk through [Lincoln's] body."

Mrs. Lincoln, who continued to wail every time she saw Clara that evening in her red-stained dress, was beside herself with grief and was taken to a parlor room in the house. About once an hour she would revisit her husband's bedside, cradling his head and blood-matted hair, and renew her inconsolable sobbing. At one point in the middle of the night, when the president's breathing took on a terrifying rattle, the First Lady screeched, letting out a "piercing cry," remembered Dr. Leale, whereupon Secretary Stanton grew livid and ordered her removal from the room. "Take that woman out and do not let her in again!" he shouted. The extended, emotional vigil had taken a toll on everyone's nerves.

The extended, emotional vigil had taken a toll on everyone's nerves.

At 6:45 a.m., with death quite near, the president's twenty-one-year-old son, Robert, a captain in the Union Army who had just returned to Washington from witnessing General Lee's surrender to General Grant at the Appomattox Court House in Virginia on April 9, effectively ending the Civil War, broke down in tears, leaning on the shoulder of Massachusetts senator Charles Sumner for support.

At 7:22 a.m., the president died. By nearly all accounts, Lincoln looked

Photograph of Mary Todd Lincoln, photographer unknown, circa 1860–65.

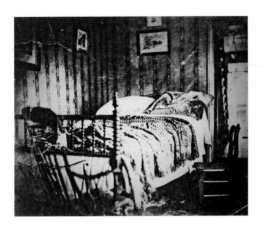

utterly at peace while breathing his final breaths. There was "no apparent suffering, no convulsive action, no rattling of the throat . . . [only] a mere cessation of breathing," noted Field. "I had never seen upon the President's face an expression more genial and pleasing." Lincoln's private secretary John Hay agreed with Field's assessment, noting that "a look of unspeakable peace came upon his worn features" at the moment of death.

Lincoln's arms were gently folded across his chest, and his eyes were closed, covered first with pennies and later with silver half-dollars (a custom likely tied to the ancient Greek practice of placing coins in or on the mouth of the deceased to bribe Charon, the mythological ferryman of the underworld, to ensure safe passage of the soul across the river Acheron to the heart of Hades, the land of the dead). Dr. Leale gingerly smoothed the president's hair, so matted with dried blood and brain matter, and everyone knelt as an emotional Secretary Stanton asked Lincoln's personal minister, Phineas Gurley, to say a prayer for the president, his family, and the country. With tears streaming down his cheeks, Stanton then, according to lore, whispered his legendary proclamation: "Now he belongs to the ages." Or to the "angels," in some accounts.[54]

AUTOPSY AND AFTERMATH

Lincoln's body was returned to the White House for an autopsy. He was transported in a hearse, accompanied by a cavalry escort, with his body laid in a simple pine crate covered with an American flag; the simplicity of the

Photograph of the room where Lincoln died, taken immediately after Lincoln's body was removed. Photo by Julius Ulke, a resident at the Petersen House.

temporary coffin suited the president, the most unpretentious chief executive in American history.

Of course, an autopsy was not needed to ascertain the cause of death—that was obvious. But it simply seemed wrong and unseemly to bury the great man with a bullet still lodged in his brain. So an autopsy ensued in the "Prince of Wales" bedroom. The guest room was so named after the British Prince of Wales who had stayed there while visiting President Buchanan in 1860.[55]

It was a poignant and painful setting for the Lincolns: their beloved eleven-year-old son, Willie, had died from a typhoid-related disease in the same elegant guest room three years earlier, on the massive, carved rosewood bed called the "Lincoln Bed" today.[56] Willie was the son most like his father, and he was, by all accounts, the president's favorite boy. He loved learning and was blessed with the president's winning personality. "He was an avid reader," notes historian Doris Kearns Goodwin, "a budding writer, and generally sweet-tempered, all reminiscent of his father."[57]

Photograph of Abraham Lincoln's funeral train in Harrisburg, Pennsylvania, by David Clark Burnite, 1865.

It seemed only fitting that both Lincolns, so much alike, would end up in the same room at the ends of their lives. In fact, they were destined to remain together for eternity: Willie's body was quickly exhumed so it could accompany his father's casket on a black garland–draped presidential funeral train, dubbed the "Lincoln Special," which largely traced in reverse Lincoln's dangerous journey to Washington for his inauguration four years earlier. Traveling seventeen hundred miles over a two-week period, the train passed through some 180 cities and 400 communities in six states plus the District of Columbia, stopping for a dozen viewing services before reaching the Oak Ridge Cemetery in Springfield, Illinois, where the president and his son were buried. One million people viewed the president's corpse; upward of seven million watched the funeral train pass by. In death as in life, Lincoln was accessible to the people, white and Black alike.[58]

In death as in life, Lincoln was accessible to the people, white and Black alike.

Army surgeons Edward Curtis and Joseph Janvier Woodward performed the autopsy on the president, whereupon Dr. Charles D. Brown followed with that miracle breakthrough in mortuary science, perfected and popularized in the North during the Civil War: embalming.[59] This key aspect of the emergent "funeral industry" that took form during the war arose from the unprecedented number of soldiers who had died in battle or from infection and disease, and in response to the many families who wanted their loved ones transported home for burial.

The improvement in embalming techniques that occurred during the war made this long-distance option increasingly possible, meaning embalmers suddenly enjoyed a lucrative business with a morbidly unlimited number of "clients." Lincoln had marveled at the embalming of his son Willie, whose body had been interred in the family vault of a Supreme Court clerk. In fact, the president visited the vault frequently over the year following Willie's death, just to glance at the face of his dead beloved son. Now, the president himself would be the recipient of this breakthrough technology.

In comparison with the body of statesman Henry Clay, whose multiple-city, train-and-steamboat burial journey in 1852 served as the model for the Lincoln funeral procession, Lincoln's corpse survived in stellar condition. Why the difference? Clay had *not* been embalmed, and his body had decayed so severely and so quickly that open-casket viewings had to be terminated during the long burial trek to his final resting place in Lexington, Kentucky. But a journey of two weeks, especially in warm spring weather, would nonetheless take its toll on even an embalmed corpse, and this was certainly the case during Lincoln's journey to Springfield. This posed a serious problem, because the ceremonies scheduled along the way were *open-casket* affairs. As one account notes, despite the embalming,

> Lincoln's shockingly black and shriveled face had needed regular powdering from Dr. Brown. His lips, as originally positioned by the undertaker, remained slightly upturned, giving him an expression of mild amusement over the commotion his passing had caused.[60]

The decomposition of Lincoln's body quickly became a topic of discussion in newspapers nationwide. In other words, not even in death could Lincoln escape the endless scrutiny that his appearance and his body seemed always, everywhere, to attract. And the more the press discussed his deteriorating corpse, the more people lined the streets for a glimpse of the president, many now motivated by mere ghoulish curiosity.

To make matters worse, Lincoln's body began emitting a putrid smell, which had to be offset with perfumes and fresh-cut flowers. In fact, flowers played such a key role in the Lincoln funeral procession that they spawned a new American tradition—the giving of flowers as a sign of condolence. As writer Richard Bak has noted,

Not even in death could Lincoln escape the endless scrutiny that his appearance and his body seemed always, everywhere, to attract.

> Previously, [flowers] had been reserved for celebrating happy occasions. But in the spring of 1865, a huge number of Americans, casting about for a way to express their

sorrow, settled on bouquets of sacrificial flowers. The sweet, melancholic perfume of lilies, lilacs, roses, and orange blossoms was everywhere that spring. It was entirely fitting that when poet Walt Whitman, who cared for wounded soldiers in Washington during the war, sat down to write of the nation's loss [upon the assassination of Lincoln], he entitled his work "When Lilacs Last in the Dooryard Bloom'd."[61]

Regarding the autopsy, hair once again masked the bullet that had shocked the world. To retrieve the projectile, the president's skull would have to be cut and opened. Dr. Curtis described the scene in a detailed letter to his mother, written a week after the procedure. "Seated around the room," he noted, "were several general officers and some civilians, silent or conversing in whispers, and to one side, stretched upon a rough framework of boards and covered only with sheets and towels, lay—cold and immovable—what but a few hours before was the soul of a great nation."[62]

The doctors began by sawing off the top of the president's head above the ears and removing just the top of the brain where the track of the bullet

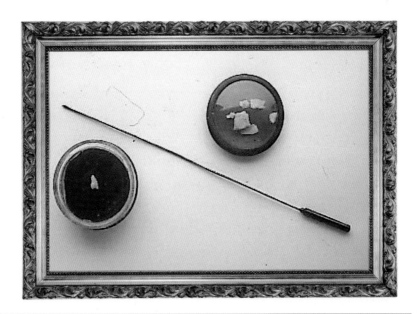

Photograph of the probe used by doctors to explore Lincoln's head wound and some fragments from his skull removed at his autopsy, from the National Museum of Health and Medicine in Washington, DC.

began. The ball, however, remained stubbornly out of view. The brain was then removed in its entirety, and while lifting the soft grayish-white mass from the skull cavity, the tiny bullet that had so dramatically changed the course of American history simply tumbled out, falling through Dr. Curtis's fingers and landing with a delicate *clink!* into an empty white basin below. The sound startled the solemn silence of the room. "There it lay upon the white china," wrote Curtis, "a little black mass not bigger than the end of my finger—dull, motionless and harmless, yet the cause of such mighty changes in the world's history as we may perhaps never realize."[63]

With the projectile recovered, the task remained to put the president's head back together as well as possible for the seemingly endless public viewings of his body to come. And despite the deterioration of the corpse that would occur in the coming weeks during the long, onerous funeral trek to Springfield, the doctors did a magnificent job of mending the president in the wake of the autopsy. Lincoln's "face wore that benignant, half-thoughtful, half-tender expression which distinguished it through life," reported journalist George Alfred Townsend. Reattaching the skull with the president's thick "mane" was necessary as well, but "the scalp was readjusted over the skull so tastefully that is seemed never to have been removed."[64]

THE RISE OF FATHER ABRAHAM

Lincoln would be deified in the decades to come—with his famous name and face adorning endless forms, from coins and currency to streets and schools and ships and public buildings of every sort. And the fact that Lincoln had been shot on Good Friday, the day of Christ's crucifixion, did not go unnoticed. Indeed, the timing of the assassination helped solidify the president's apotheosis as "Father Abraham," the foremost sacrificial servant in American history who had given everything, even his life, so the country could survive and live in peace.

But in the period immediately after Lincoln's assassination, beautifying the president and polishing his image were neither necessary nor desired by most Americans. In fact, the opposite feeling prevailed, for remembering the unruly-haired giant, warts and all—by viewing the slain president not as a god or a secular saint, but as an imperfect man who had struggled and persevered his way to greatness, despite mighty obstacles—helped Americans come to terms with the tragedy in a more personal and meaningful way.

The president's homespun manners and unkempt looks, casual affability, and easy accessibility to the public (a habit that eventually cost him his life, but which endeared him to the people) only underscored the humility and sheer commonness from which Americans of all races and social classes could glean inspiration. Being "one of them" as well as "among them" served only to magnify for the masses the extraordinary way Lincoln had navigated a most improbable path in life.

> *Being "one of them" as well as "among them" served only to magnify for the masses the extraordinary way Lincoln had navigated a most improbable path in life.*

Although fated with a pedigree unpromising and unmoneyed, this most self-made of self-made men had risen from poverty to the presidency with dogged resolve and a belief in his destiny that his law partner William Herndon likened to "a little engine that knew no rest."[65] In other words, Lincoln had mastered the ability to soldier on, with patience and purpose, against all odds, through crisis after crisis, often forlorn but not defeated, living to fight another day on yet another front until finally reaching the hallowed realm where he resides today: as the Savior of the Union, the Great Emancipator of the enslaved, and, to many, the greatest president in American history.

Lincoln's craggy looks and shaggy-haired homeliness merely burnished this perception of his common-man greatness. In fact, Lincoln's homely appearance has even been tied to one of the most steadfast tenets of the American psyche: the belief in American exceptionalism. "Lincoln made people care about [his appearance] by tying it to their national saga," writes historian Richard Fox. "Only in America was self-making possible on such a grand scale, he kept saying, and only in America, was a man like him—of such unprepossessing origins, in appearance and social standing—able to rise to such heights of power and respect."[66]

In the end, Lincoln needed no makeover to prove his worthiness for inclusion in history's pantheon of heroes who had changed the world. Quite the opposite was true, as a December 28, 1866, story in the *New-York Tribune* rather poetically made clear:

> People do not want a "nice" portrait, nor a "handsome" portrait, nor an "ideal" portrait [of Lincoln]. They want to say, this is the man who suffered and died in our cause. Let flatterers stand aside, and squeamish people. Show us the grim features, the shaggy head, the beetling brow, the big nose, the great mouth. What do we care for his homeliness? His soul transfigures this scarred and craggy face as sunset strikes against a mountain side, and changes rugged cliff, and black ravine, and darkest wood into golden or rosy cloud.[67]

W. E. B. Du Bois, one of the foremost African American leaders of the early twentieth century, echoed these sentiments but sang Lincoln's virtues in a simpler, pithier way. "I love [Lincoln] not because he was perfect," he explained, "but because he was not and yet triumphed."[68]

The Last Hours of Abraham Lincoln, 1868. Designed by John B. Bachelder and painted by Alonzo Chappel, this work of art depicts those who visited the dying president throughout the night and early morning of April 14–15, 1865. These people did not visit Lincoln at the same time; they could not have all fit in the small first-floor room of the Petersen House. In fact, artists inserted so many dignitaries in their later renditions of the death scene that the narrow section of the boardinghouse where Lincoln lay was dubbed the "Rubber Room" for its endless elasticity. Lincoln's wife, Mary, is pictured in the center, lying across the president's body. His son Robert stands in the foreground to the right of the bed. Vice President Andrew Johnson is seated at the far left.

CHAPTER TWO

LOCKS AND PRESIDENTIAL LEGACIES

THE LONG, LUSH HISTORY OF

Collecting Hair

*I*f hair was intimately entwined with the life and assassination of Abraham Lincoln and the end of his presidency, all were intimately tied to the start of another presidency—that of Theodore Roosevelt (26th US president, 1901–09).

Upon the death of William McKinley (25th US president, 1897–1901) on September 14, 1901, from the wounds he had suffered eight days earlier when he was shot by a deranged anarchist at the Pan-American Exposition in Buffalo, New York, Roosevelt became the third vice president to assume the presidency due to assassination. He also became the youngest president in American history. Roosevelt was only forty-two years old, and like the dashing Boston blue blood fifty-nine years later (John F. Kennedy, 35th US president, 1961–63) who became, at age forty-three, the youngest *elected* US president, Roosevelt's robust youth and dynamic personality would revolutionize the public perception of the presidency.

Death, Lincoln, and hair would all play roles in Roosevelt's ascent to the White House in 1901 and election to the presidency in his own right in 1904. In fact, Roosevelt's first encounter with any aspect of the US presidency may have been at age six, when he peered out of an upstairs window of his grandfather's Union Square mansion and witnessed Lincoln's coffin below as it was carried along Broadway during the funeral procession's stopover in New York on April 24–25, 1865. A photo in the New-York Historical Society even shows the little Roosevelt in the window. It's an extraordinary moment in history for a camera to capture, enveloping both the end time of one president and the likely spiritual birth of another. For was this the very moment in time that set Roosevelt's presidential imagination alight, forever altering the character and course of his life and American history? "It is not too much to imagine," muses presidential historian

> It's an extraordinary moment in history for a camera to capture, enveloping both the end time of one president and the likely spiritual birth of another.

Michael Beschloss, "that this photograph may have captured the moment that kindled [Roosevelt's] ambition to emulate the Great Emancipator."[69]

Lincoln had long fascinated Roosevelt and served as a source of inspiration for him. Busts and portraits of the famed president adorned Roosevelt's manse at Sagamore Hill, New York, and both men, personally and politically, had a strong appreciation for nature, central government, and individual rights; both also were raconteurs *par excellence*.

Roosevelt's friendship with Lincoln's personal secretary, the magnificently mustachioed John Hay (who had a close relationship with Lincoln and had

The Procession Approaching Union Square, photograph taken April 25, 1865, depicts Abraham Lincoln's funeral procession on Broadway heading toward Union Square. The building on the left is the home of Cornelius Van Schaack Roosevelt, grandfather of Theodore Roosevelt; one of the two children in the open window in the upper left is believed to be young Theodore.

known Theodore's beloved father) only underscored this connection with past greatness. After Lincoln's assassination, Hay held several diplomatic posts abroad in the late 1860s, began a multivolume biography of Lincoln with fellow Lincoln secretary John Nicolay in the 1870s, and traveled the world in the 1880s as an editorial writer for the *New-York Tribune*, before serving as US ambassador to Great Britain in 1897–98 and then as US secretary of state from 1898 to 1905.

Young Roosevelt and Hay had corresponded during the latter's newspaper years, but it was amid their joint government service during the McKinley administration that the men became especially acquainted. In fact, one of the most famous lines ever penned about any war in history issued from Hay to Roosevelt at the end of the Spanish-American War of 1898, the conflict that made Roosevelt—as leader of the famed Rough Riders cavalry unit—a national hero and the United States a world power and imperial state. "It has been a splendid little war," an ebullient Hay blithely quipped to Roosevelt about the hundred-day conflict, which, not so blithely, had left thousands dead.[70]

Hay offered him his cherished "Lincoln ring."

Hay and Roosevelt had a father-son relationship, which both enjoyed and valued. When the "son," twenty years younger, became president in 1901, the "father" was asked to remain on as US secretary of state, which Hay did, and his poise, polish, and sober statesmanship served as a stabilizing force for the

Portrait of John Hay, by photographer C. M. Gilbert, circa 1904.

brash new chief executive fond of rocking the world with his "Big Stick" diplomacy. But in the fall of 1904, when Roosevelt was elected to the presidency in his own right, Hay's health was failing. With his days, professionally and personally, clearly nigh over, and Roosevelt just hitting his stride, Hay offered the pup president one of his prized possessions, something very dear to him that Roosevelt could wear on Inauguration Day, March 4, 1905. Hay offered him his cherished "Lincoln ring." And why was it special? The gold, oval ring contained a lock of Lincoln's hair.

HAIR COLLECTING: A POPULAR PASTIME

Collecting hair may sound bizarre, even macabre, to the modern reader, but the pastime is alive and well today, especially in our era of celebrity obsession. "People are interested in owning a piece of history and a piece of famous people,"[71] says documents expert John Reznikoff, who is credited by *Guinness World Records* with owning the world's largest collection of celebrity hair, from more than 150 luminaries, including Marilyn Monroe (whose famed coif, he told me, had been clipped and collected by many, including her embalmer).

In fact, hair collection is big business. Auctions the world over routinely sell follicles of the famous—for the right price, of course. Hair from the "King," Elvis Presley, sold for an impressive $115,000 in 2002, with a single strand selling for more than $1,000 in 2009. Surprisingly, even more expensive were tresses from revolutionary leader "Che" Guevara, whose hair sold in 2007 for the very nonproletarian price of $119,500, though thrown in with the hair were photographs of the radical, a set of his fingerprints, and maps used in tracking him down. Not all such auctions are successful, though. In 2007, after Britney Spears notoriously shaved her head, the owner of the California salon where the rash shearing took place offered the pile of hair clippings on eBay for a shocking $1 million. Despite the ancillary items thrown in with the lopped locks—the clippers Britney used, a blue lighter left behind by

In fact, hair collection is big business.

the singer, and a half-drunk can of Red Bull that the star had sipped on—no one paid the million, and the auction was suspended.[72]

Hair collecting is not, however, exclusive to the celebrity-obsessed present—it has a history both rich and riveting. As one of the most durable components of the human body, stubbornly resistant to decomposition, hair has long been seen as a reliable vehicle for preserving the past and memorializing our loved ones across time, and the impulse behind collecting hair is the same one that generates the popularity of memorial jewelry today. Necklaces, rings, bracelets, and pendants imprinted with the fingerprints, footprints, lip prints, and handwriting of our loved ones, or even containing the ashes of the deceased—all are intimate keepsakes and tangible, unique ways of remaining in touch, *literally*, with the individuals we cherish and dearly miss. A company in Chicago, LifeGem, will even make diamonds from the ashes and hair of your lost loved one. In 2009 the company announced its intention to create ten half-carat diamonds from the carbon in the hair of Michael Jackson, giving a diamond to each of Jackson's children. It had previously made diamonds out of the hair of Beethoven (reportedly selling them for some $200,000) and will even make gems from the fur of your favorite pet.[73]

Contrary to what readers might think today, asking for a snippet of someone's hair was historically considered a gesture of respect. "More so than an autograph, it was a sign of affection," says Harry R. Rubenstein, a Lincoln scholar and curator emeritus at the National

Portrait of George Washington, oil on canvas, painted by artist Gilbert Stuart, 1803.

Museum of American History.[74] Union College librarian John Myers likens the custom to "the selfies of the day."[75] Myers made headlines in 2018 after finding, nestled between the pages of a 1793 almanac, an envelope containing locks of George Washington's hair. For the owner of the almanac, says Myers, the book storing his precious keepsake was "like his iPhone."[76]

Hair collecting was especially popular in the Victorian era, which exhibited a morbid obsession with the end of life that some have labeled a "cult of death." Victorians, for instance, developed elaborate customs for how to mourn properly: for how long to mourn, what to wear when mourning, and the proper colors to wear; for why drapes should be drawn (for private mourning), mirrors covered (so mourners can't see themselves while mourning), and the hands of clocks stopped (so the soul won't linger in human time and haunt the living instead of leaving for the afterworld); for why it's smart to carry a dead body feet first out of a house (so the deceased can't glance back and beckon the living to the world of the dead); for why burying a corpse with a rope attached to a bell outside the grave might also be wise—for ringing for help (thus, "saved by the bell") in case the corpse proved to be not really dead or, Lazarus-like, sprang miraculously back to life.

Frequently tied to these mourning customs was that tangible, ever-personal element of hair. For example, locks from the deceased were often preserved in rings, lockets, pendants, brooches, buttons, watch fobs, shirt studs, and the like. Such "mourning jewelry" was a continuation of sorts of the *memento mori* craze of the sixteenth and seventeenth centuries, when jewelry was popularly adorned with skulls, coffins, hourglasses, and crossbones to remind the wearers of the fleeting nature of time ("*Memento mori*"—Latin, "Remember, you must die") and to spur them to live a virtuous life. Hair was also used for "mourning art," in which locks from the deceased were woven into rings distributed at the funeral; chopped into a fine powder and mixed with paint for the creation of mourning scenes; or used for the hair on an

Contrary to what readers might think today, asking for a snippet of someone's hair was historically considered a gesture of respect.

"Hair is
at once the
most delicate
and lasting
of our
materials,
and survives
us like love."

"effigy doll," if the deceased was a child—the doll would be displayed during the funeral and then laid on the child's grave site.

Highly popular, too, were memorial wreaths, in which the lost loved one's hair was intertwined with wire and flowers and displayed in the home as a kind of "family tree," conveying one's ancestry through the ages. "Hair is at once the most delicate and lasting of our materials, and survives us like love," reported *Godey's Lady's Book* in 1860, a publication that frequently published patterns for creating hair wreaths. "So light, so gentle," it added, "so escaping from the idea of death, that, with a lock of hair belonging to a child or friend, we may almost look up to heaven and compare notes with angelic nature—may almost say: 'I have a piece of thee here, not unworthy of thy being now.'"[77] By the late nineteenth century, hair wreaths had become common exhibition items at county fairs, where they were judged in contests, and in the early twentieth century, hair jewelry was even mass-marketed through the ubiquitous Sears, Roebuck and Co. catalog. But such hair relics, by this time, were clearly declining in popularity, as another, more exacting method of remembering our loved ones was becoming increasingly affordable and available to the masses: photography.

THE DARK SIDE OF HAIR COLLECTIONS

Perhaps not surprising, some unsavory chapters exist in the long history of hair collection. The black clump of Michael Jackson's hair, fished out of a dirty shower drain at the Carlyle Hotel in New York in the 1980s and sold at auction in 2011 for nearly $11,000, is one such example. (The winning bidder, a gambling website, planned to "immortalize" the pop star by inserting his hair in a roulette ball that could be licensed to casinos for special occasions.) The following year, a hairy remnant from the dead body of notorious gangster John

Dillinger, along with other crime memorabilia, sold at auction for $5,513; the auction winner, however, won not locks from the killer's head, but a single mustache hair snagged by the mold of his postmortem death mask.[78]

Creepier still is the novel wig and hair collection of England's King Charles II. Charles's reign (1660–85) marked the beginning of the Restoration period in English history, when the monarchy was restored after a decade of austere Puritan rule. In contrast to the short and simple haircuts of the Puritan era ("Roundheads," the Puritans were called, due to their cropped hairstyles), the Restoration period was a time of elaborate wig wearing and licentiousness of every sort; gambling, drinking, and carnality of all stripes flourished unencumbered, and erotic clubs sprang up like mushrooms after rain in reaction to the prudishness of the former regime.

Charles gladly contributed to the era's louche and libertine ways. Called the

Photograph of a nineteenth-century hair wreath, Clara Barkley Dorr House museum, Pensacola, Florida.

"Merry Monarch" for the rakish frivolity of his court, Charles had mistresses aplenty (including the witty and irresistible Nell Gwyn, one of England's first actresses and comediennes), along with a dozen or so out-of-wedlock children. In fact, the king's twin passions for women and wigs intersected in interesting ways. First, because thinning and graying hair were common signs of syphilis, Charles's adoption of the foppish French fetish for wig wearing (especially long,

Portrait of King Charles II, oil on canvas, painted by artist John Michael Wright, circa 1670s.

ringlet-laden wigs of natural color) could well have stemmed from his early baldness and desire to hide the effects of an STD.

A more startling connection between the two is the hair he collected for the wig created in honor of his many *inamoratas*—a memorial of sorts to their "contributions" to the monarchy. However, it wasn't hair from the heads of his mistresses that he collected, but hair from their . . . nether regions. The resulting "pubic hair wig" became a highly coveted curio, revered by and stolen through the centuries by assorted male clubs in Scotland.[79]

However, it wasn't hair from the heads of his mistresses that he collected, but hair from their . . . nether regions.

MEMORIALIZING LINCOLN

Hair and blood relics were common in the wake of Lincoln's assassination. In fact, after Lincoln's death, there was "a rush to find mementos of anything Lincoln touched or gave that was personal," says historian and curator Harry R. Rubenstein.[80]

Immediately after Lincoln's body was removed from the Petersen House on the morning of April 15 and transported to the White House, two boarders, brothers Henry and Julius Ulke, who operated a portrait studio on Pennsylvania Avenue, set up a tripod and photographed the president's death room for posterity. The mad scramble for physical mementos then began, as citizens stripped the Petersen House and Ford's Theatre of anything and everything tied to the tragedy. The situation became so frenzied that troops had to be called in to restore order.

At the Petersen House, torn pieces of Lincoln's clothing and especially his bedsheets and pillows—all blood soaked—were taken by residents of the house for either personal collections or later sales. William "Willie" Clark, the boarder who was out for the evening on the night the president was shot and whose bedroom was used to care for the dying president, was obviously in a prime position to secure relics of the historic event. Upon his return to his room, he immediately saved samples of the bed linen laden with the president's brain matter. He also had Lincoln's boots and clothes, which he could have kept but instead graciously returned to the president's son.

Clark then battled a constant barrage of souvenir hunters. "Since the death of our president hundreds daily call at the house to gain admission to my room," he wrote in a letter to his sister, four days after the president's death. "Everybody has a great desire to obtain some memento from my room so that whoever comes in has to be closely watched for fear that they will steal something." Eerily, after the president's body was removed from his bed on April 15, Willie proceeded to sleep in it, that very night. "The same mattrass [sic] is on my bed, and the same coverlit [sic] covers me nightly that covered him while dying," he wrote.[81]

Assorted artifacts and blood relics from that fateful night have been widely dispersed since then. For example, the Chicago History Museum acquired Lincoln's deathbed, along with the First Lady's blood-stained black velvet cloak. The Henry Ford Museum in Michigan has the red-silk walnut rocking chair from Ford's Theatre that the president was sitting in when he was shot. Ford's Theatre has the single-shot Derringer pistol used to shoot the president, the knife Booth used to slice Major Rathbone, one of the assassin's boots, Booth's diary, a chair from the president's theater box that evening, one of the bloody pillows from the Petersen House, and the custom-made Brooks Brothers overcoat Lincoln wore during the assassination (now with a severed left sleeve, due to the blood-soaked lining that had been cut away and divvied up for mementos over the years). And the National Museum of Health and Medicine in Silver Spring, Maryland, has bone fragments from the president's skull, the flattened Derringer ball that killed the president, the long Nélaton probe used to explore the path of the bullet, and even the bloodstained cuffs cut from the shirt Dr. Edward Curtis wore while assisting with the autopsy.[82]

But by far the most acquired memento tied to the assassinated president was *hair*. Perhaps the first person to collect Lincoln's tresses after the shooting was Dr. Joseph K. Barnes, the surgeon general and one of the many doctors at the Petersen House tending to the president. He collected the hair while Lincoln was still alive, securing about thirty strands and sealing them in an envelope with a note that read, "Hair removed from the head of President Lincoln April 14th 65 in examination of the wound"; the hair was sold at a Dallas auction in 2015 for $25,000, part of the larger auction of Lincoln memorabilia that day that fetched an astounding $803,889.[83]

But by far the most acquired memento tied to the assassinated president was hair.

Secretary of War Edwin Stanton acquired an even larger sample of Lincoln's locks during a quiet moment alone with the president on the morning of April 15, before Lincoln's body was transported to the White House; Dr. C. H. Liebermann, also present throughout the death vigil, clipped and collected the president's hair as well. Stanton sealed the hair he snipped in an envelope, addressing it "For Mrs. Welles," the wife of Navy Secretary Gideon Welles. Mary Jane Welles was one of Mary Todd Lincoln's closest friends, and both women had bonded over shared grief and consoled each other in the wake of tragic deaths—after the death of eleven-year-old Willie Lincoln in 1862 and the passing of the Welleses' three-year-old son the following year. Upon receiving the envelope, Mrs. Welles labeled it with the note, "Lock of Mr. Lincoln's hair April 15, 1865, M.J.W." She later mounted the locks in an oval gold frame, along with flowers collected and dried from the president's funeral. A note on the back of the frame reads, "Sacred to the Memory of Abraham Lincoln 16th President of the United States." Willie Clark, in whose bed the president had died, secured a lock of the president's hair as well, "which I have neatly framed," he later noted.[84]

Additional hair was clipped from the president at his autopsy on April 15. Lincoln's personal physician, Robert Stone, cut several chunks of the presidential locks, some for Mrs. Lincoln, who had requested them from a room across

the hall from where the autopsy took place. Dr. Charles Taft, also present for the procedure, received some as well, including "a lock stained with blood," he noted. However, army doctor Robert Reyburn, who was also present at the autopsy, "very urgently pleaded" for a sample of Lincoln's hair and was denied his request. But after a clump of Lincoln's locks fell to the floor amid the rash clipping and collecting, Reyburn "seized upon the precious relic at once." Also receiving a considerable hair sample was Dr. Lyman Beecher Todd, the First Lady's cousin. He packaged the keepsake in the only thing he had in his pocket at the time—a War Department telegram sent just after news of the assassination. "He wrapped the lock, stained with blood or brain fluid, in this telegram and hastily wrote on it in pencil: 'Hair of A. Lincoln,'" noted Dr. Todd's son. The precious strands and telegram were stored for decades, until finally sold at auction in 2020 for more than $81,000.[85]

After the autopsy, famed Civil War photographer Alexander Gardner received about twenty-five strands of Lincoln's hair, cut by one of the undertakers who had cared for Lincoln's body; the locks sold for $6,250 in 2018. Lincoln's embalmer also collected some hair samples, distributing a few strands to the soldier guarding the room; they, too, were eventually sold at auction. But

This studio portrait features a well-dressed Mrs. Lincoln holding young Tad's hand while Willie stands to the left, hat in hand, circa 1860, just two years before Willie's death.

a highly unusual troika of Lincoln-related hair relics was sold in 2016, when offered for sale were strands of Lincoln's hair, a sampling of Booth's locks that were extracted at his autopsy (opening bid: $25,000), and—most bizarre—a log cabin modeled out of . . . still more of Lincoln's hair.[86]

Given the widespread scalping of Lincoln in the wake of the assassination, it's surprising that, at the open-casket services for Lincoln that followed across the country, the public didn't encounter a bald sixteenth president.

He packaged the keepsake in the only thing he had in his pocket at the time—a War Department telegram sent just after news of the assassination.

HAY'S PRESIDENTIAL HAIR GIFTING

Roosevelt's mentor and father figure, John Hay, also ended up with some of Lincoln's hair. In fact, he wanted this intimate memento of the slain president so badly that he paid one hundred dollars for just a few fine strands—equivalent to thousands of dollars today. Like reverent Christians of the Middle Ages who preserved the bones and organs of martyred saints in special reliquaries, Hay preserved and displayed his precious relic in a special way, too, in this case under glass, in the setting of a ring—the very ring he gave to Theodore Roosevelt to wear at his inauguration on March 4, 1905.

Strangely, though paradigmatic of the hair-relic craze of the day, this was actually the *third* time that Hay had gifted a hair ring to a US president. The first time was after the presidential election of 1876, one of the most contentious and disputed elections in American history. After Rutherford B. Hayes was finally declared the victor, beating Samuel J. Tilden by a single electoral vote, becoming the nineteenth US president, Hay

sent the president-elect a congratulatory gift: a gold ring encasing hair from the man who had pioneered the position of president, George Washington. Hay had received the icon's hair from the son of Alexander Hamilton. "Hayes was extremely touched by this talismanic link to the nation's first president," notes biographer John Taliaferro. "It will be difficult to wear [the ring] at all times," replied the new president to Hay, "but I shall prize it, and will wear it on special occasions if not constantly."[87]

The *second* instance occurred twenty years later, right after the election of 1896, when William McKinley won the election handily and became the nation's twenty-fifth president. Once again, Hay sent a congratulatory gift to the president-elect—yet another gold ring containing still more hair from the head of George Washington. Like President Hayes before him, McKinley was deeply moved by the gift and "began wearing the ring immediately."[88]

The *third* instance of Hay's presidential hair gifting was in 1905, with his present to Theodore Roosevelt. This ring— the Lincoln ring—was exceptionally special, to both the giver and the given. "Please wear [this ring] tomorrow," wrote Hay

Top: gold ring (top and side view) containing hair from George Washington, given by John Hay to Rutherford B. Hayes when the latter became president in 1877. **Bottom:** gold ring containing hair from Abraham Lincoln, given by John Hay to President Theodore Roosevelt to wear on Inauguration Day, March 4, 1905.

to Roosevelt. "The hair in this ring is from the head of Abraham Lincoln. Dr. Taft cut it off the night of the assassination, and I got it from his son," he explained. "You are one of the men who most thoroughly understand and appreciate Lincoln. I have had your monogram and Lincoln's engraved on the ring."[89]

Like presidents Hayes and McKinley before him, Roosevelt was deeply moved by the intimate gift. "Dear John," he replied, "Surely no other President, on the eve of his inauguration, has ever received such a gift from such a friend." (Hay must have chuckled at this line.) "I am wearing the ring now; I shall think of it and you as I take the oath tomorrow." The *Washington Post* noticed the new president's special jewelry the next day, in its coverage of the inauguration. "On the third finger of President Roosevelt's left hand during the inaugural ceremonies was a heavily embossed gold seal ring," it reported, a ring containing "a lock of hair cut from the head of Abraham Lincoln just after the assassination, and before his death."[90]

Although Hay's hair gifting was not the unique gesture that each presidential recipient imagined, the rings were special nonetheless, and their connection with past greatness had a powerful impact on each leader. The "Lincoln ring" in particular had a lasting influence on Roosevelt, affecting both his perception of the presidency and how he discharged his duties as president. "When I wore [the] ring," he noted in his *Autobiography* in 1913, "I bound myself more than ever to treat the Constitution, after the manner of Abraham Lincoln, as a document which put human rights above property rights when the two conflicted."[91]

The "Lincoln ring" in particular had a lasting influence on Roosevelt.

MEMORIALIZING WASHINGTON

As suggested by two of the three rings presented to presidents by John Hay (gifts which contained hair from George Washington), this national obsession with White House tresses didn't begin with Lincoln and his assassination but rather started with the adoration and memorializing of the very first president.

The similarities between the two leaders are striking, especially in how the public responded to each president and to each man's death. In both cases, each president experienced an apotheosis, rising to near-sainthood status, and in each instance in each century, hair figured as the chief treasure and talisman by which the public revered their hero, honored his memory, showed their patriotic pride, and remained connected—in a physical, tactile way— with the great leader and his legacy. In fact, such relics were considered a filiopietistic status symbol of great value.

"Americans for most of the century that followed Washington's death craved physical vouchers of their fallen hero," writes Robert McCracken Peck, a senior fellow at and the curator of arts and artifacts of the Academy of Natural Sciences at Drexel University. "Second only to his autographs, the most widely distributed relics of the first president are pieces of his hair." According to historian Keith Beutler, more than a hundred institutions—from museums to universities—own locks of Washington's hair. "There's no one whose hair survives to that extent," notes Beutler. "It's just surreal how much interest there was." And this keen interest continues today. In 2021 a sample of Washington's hair, encased in a brass-and-glass locket, opened at auction for $1,000 and sold, forty-five bids later, for $39,921. A similar lock of Washington's hair sold for $35,763 in 2019.[92]

"Second only to his autographs, the most widely distributed relics of the first president are pieces of his hair."

Washington's hair is intriguing on many levels, not least because of the important political and symbolic messages conveyed by his tresses and how he styled them. Contrary to popular belief, Washington did not—like so many leaders in the eighteenth century—wear a wig. Perukes (or periwigs, as male wigs were called) were widely associated with monarchy and nobility, which Washington, as the commander of America's revolutionary forces, was busy rebelling against, and so on a philosophical level he opposed elaborate wigs as the pompous trappings of an anti-republican social order. *White* hair, however, remained a fashionable sign of wealth and significance, and so Washington gladly powdered his slicked-back, yanked-tight, reddish-brown locks (which had faded to grayish white by the time of his presidency)—hence the widespread misconception that Washington donned a white wig.

But Washington's style, even with his powdering and prominent pigtail (a "queue," sometimes worn in a small bag to prevent the powder from messing up one's clothes) and perfectly poofed curls that bracketed his neck, remained strikingly more simple and populist than the style of England's leader during the American Revolution, King George III, whose powdered perukes, ermine robes, and pearl- and diamond-encrusted crowns of gold stood him in stark contrast to the relatively unpretentious leader of the upstart Americans.

Given Washington's prominence and the popularity of hair collecting in his day, it is not surprising that the famed, victorious commander of the Revolutionary War and historic first president of the new United States was asked incessantly for samples of his locks. It is also not surprising, given his chivalrous nature, that Washington felt obliged as a gentleman to accommodate these appeals. What *is*

Portrait of George Washington, drawn by John George Wood and engraved by William Satchwell Leney, circa 1814.

shocking, though, is that Washington even honored these requests during the darkest days of the war.

For example, amid the often miserable half-year camp at Valley Forge (1777–78), while suffering frigid temperatures, insufficient food, and rampant disease, where the bare feet of bootless soldiers left bloody footprints in the snow and men slept on filthy straw riddled with maggots and lice, conditions that would decimate one-sixth of Washington's army (two thousand men)—even in the midst of all this, at a time of supreme crisis of national survival, the American leader still mustered the time and energy to answer . . . *an appeal for his hair.* The request came from the daughter of New Jersey governor William Livingston, and in a return letter to her dated March 18, 1778, Washington enclosed the requested sample of his locks. "General Washington having been informed of the honor done him by Miss Kitty Livingston in wishing for a lock of his Hair," he wrote, "takes the liberty of enclosing one, accompanied by his most respectful compliments."[93]

Clearly, Washington was an obliging participant in the hair-collecting craze. A 1789 receipt exists for his payment to a New York jeweler for "hair work put into a breast pin" for Mrs. Washington. A decade later, at the end of his presidency, there was even a hair-related ceremony that became a standard story in nineteenth-century biographies of Washington:

Even in the midst of all this, at a time of supreme crisis of national survival, the American leader still mustered the time and energy to answer . . . an appeal for his hair.

Photograph of a snuffbox containing a lock of George Washington's hair, collector unknown, circa 1800–10.

On leaving the seat of Government after the inauguration of his successor, Washington presented to all his principal officers some token of regard. When Mrs. Oliver Wolcott, the wife of one of these gentlemen [Treasury Secretary Oliver Wolcott] and the particular friend and correspondent . . . called "to take leave," Mrs. Washington asked if she did not wish a memorial of the General. "Yes," replied Mrs. Wolcott, "I should like a lock of his hair." Mrs. Washington instantly took her scissors, and with a happy smile, cut a large lock from her husband's head, added it to one from her own, and presented them to her fair friend.[94]

It seems even in his will, Washington made provisions for meeting the constant demand for his valuable locks. Five female family members and friends should receive "a mourning Ring of the value of one hundred dollars," he stipulated, rings that likely contained or were accompanied by strands of his hair.[95]

A steady supply of Washington's hair continued to be available even after the president's death. Washington's assistant, Tobias Lear, admits to cutting locks of Washington's hair right after the president was laid in his coffin, likely doing so both to acquire a memento for himself and to prepare for the deluge of hair-related requests that was certain to come. And come they did, including one to Mrs. Washington in January 1800 from the legendary Paul Revere, who asked for a lock of Washington's hair on behalf of the Masons' Grand Lodge of the Commonwealth of Massachusetts.[96]

> A steady supply of Washington's hair continued to be available even after the president's death.

According to *Antiques* magazine, the legendary silversmith and patriot even promised to fashion a miniature golden urn to hold the "invaluable relique [sic] of the Hero and the Patriot whom Their wishes would immortalize." Lear replied on behalf of the First Lady, who consented to the gift.[97]

Washington's barber, Martin Pierie, was also a prominent source of posthumous locks from the president. The barber reportedly amassed quite a stash of clippings from the famed leader's noggin and even leveraged his collection in the marketing of his barbering services after the president's death. Many samples of Washington's hair that have circulated since then have a provenance traceable to either Lear or Pierie.

HAIR COLLECTIONS LIVE ON, WITH CONTROVERSY

Two early-nineteenth-century curio collectors and promoters of public knowledge were especially instrumental in feeding this fascination with presidential tresses that continues to this day.

One was John Varden (circa 1790–1865), a talented and peripatetic theater set designer whose frequent travels enabled him to amass a vast array of stuff, both serious and silly. He had Egyptian mummies, historic coins, intriguing fossils, Native American tools, and drawings from famed Renaissance artist Albrecht Dürer, as well as fish heads, a jackal, a bat, a pig with two heads and three ears, a ball of hair from a dam in Cooperstown, New York, and an English musket ball extracted from his brother's shoulder. To display his burgeoning gallimaufry of curiosities, he opened a public gallery in his home, calling it the "Washington Museum," in 1836. A showman at heart, Varden and his museum overlapped in time with perhaps the most famous showman ever to live, P. T. Barnum, who took over the American Museum in New York City in 1841.[98] But most precious to Varden was his collection of hair, which included locks from inventor Samuel F. B. Morse, generals Winfield Scott and Sam Houston, senators Henry Clay and Jefferson Davis, and, most significantly, all fourteen presidents to date, from George Washington to Franklin Pierce. His wood-framed "Hair of the Presidents" display, along with other items from his collection, was eventually acquired by the National Institute for the Promotion of Science, which displayed its relics

But most precious to Varden was his collection of hair, which included locks from inventor Samuel F. B. Morse.

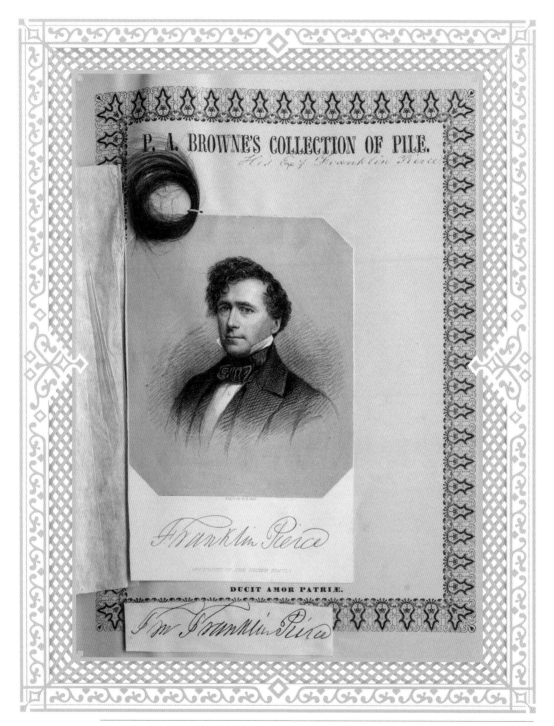

A sample of President Franklin Pierce's hair, from the collection of Peter A. Browne, circa 1840s–50s.

at the National Gallery of the US Patent Office, and then by the Smithsonian Institution, where Varden worked from 1858 until his death.

A second purveyor of presidential tresses was Philadelphia attorney and naturalist Peter Arrell Browne (1782–1860). Yet another eccentric collector of the day, Browne amassed a wide assortment of botanical and geological specimens before turning his attention to wool, fur, and eventually human hair. By collecting, as he described it, "locks of hair or wool of the heads of persons of all nations, races, sects, and varieties," he sought to understand the rich diversity of life in a pre-DNA era.[99]

This attention to biological "varieties," however, often meant focusing on the bizarre, reflecting the nineteenth century's obsession with exoticism and "human curiosities." African slave Sarah Baartman, for example, was put on display and objectified in Europe and England in the 1810s because of her abnormally large buttocks (likely due to a condition known as steatopygia); marketed as the "Hottentot Venus," she was even sexually abused by paying crowds.[100] The severely deformed Joseph Merrick, aka the "Elephant Man," who likely suffered from the very rare Proteus syndrome (an extreme overgrowth of muscle, bones, skin, and tissue), was similarly marketed by London showmen in the 1880s. Both are prime examples, along with the rise of the creepy carnival "freak show," of this strange period of curiosity and exploitation.

Both are prime examples, along with the rise of the creepy carnival "freak show," of this strange period of curiosity and exploitation.

In keeping with these times, Browne's hair collection was equally eclectic, including hair from "dwarfs and giants," fetuses at different stages of gestation, corpses, a centenarian, and even a convicted murderer (before and after his hanging); from Chang and Eng Bunker, the original "Siamese Twins"

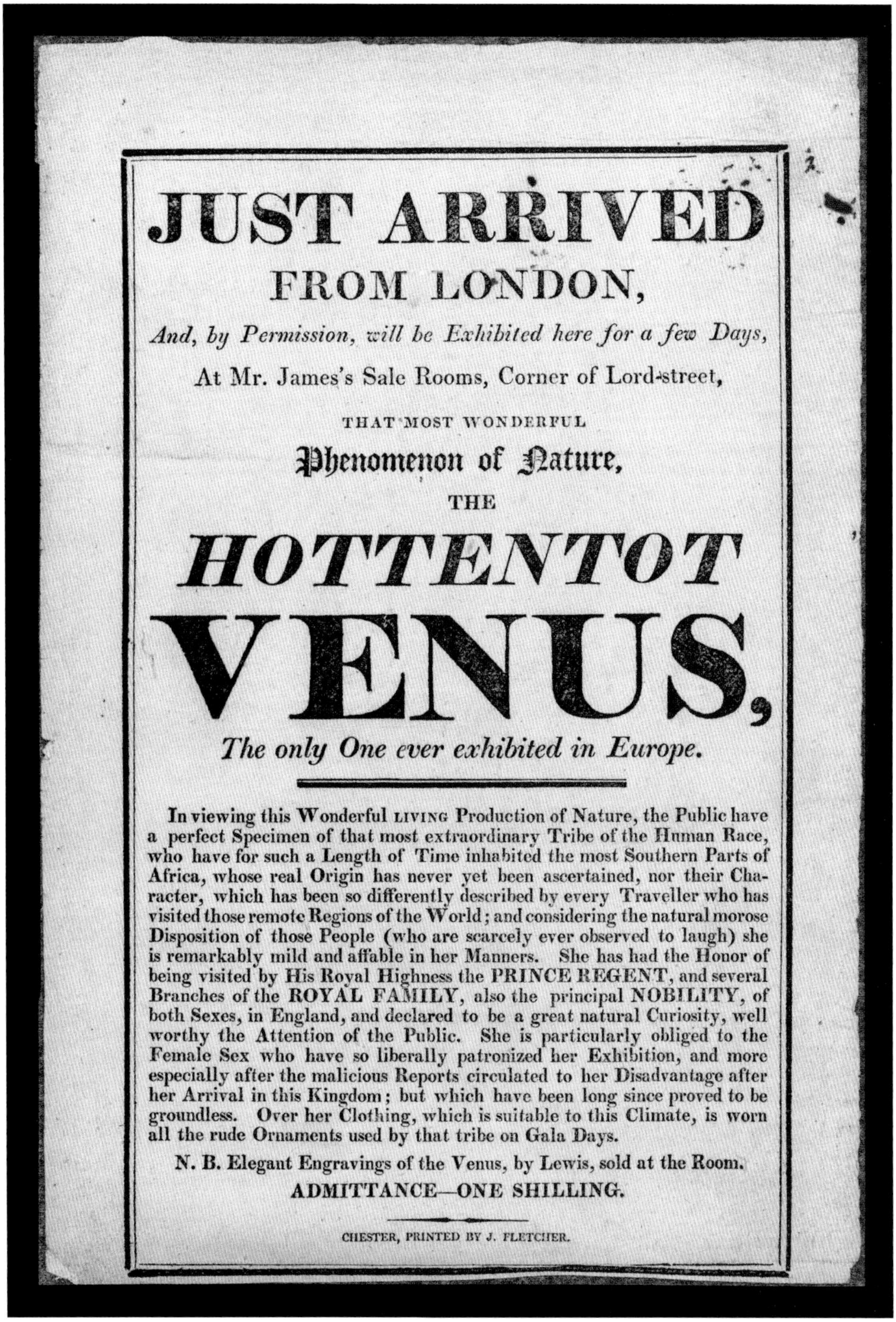

JUST ARRIVED

FROM LONDON,

And, by Permission, will be Exhibited here for a few Days,

At Mr. James's Sale Rooms, Corner of Lord-street,

THAT MOST WONDERFUL

Phenomenon of Nature,

THE

HOTTENTOT

VENUS,

The only One ever exhibited in Europe.

In viewing this Wonderful LIVING Production of Nature, the Public have a perfect Specimen of that most extraordinary Tribe of the Human Race, who have for such a Length of Time inhabited the most Southern Parts of Africa, whose real Origin has never yet been ascertained, nor their Character, which has been so differently described by every Traveller who has visited those remote Regions of the World; and considering the natural morose Disposition of those People (who are scarcely ever observed to laugh) she is remarkably mild and affable in her Manners. She has had the Honor of being visited by His Royal Highness the PRINCE REGENT, and several Branches of the ROYAL FAMILY, also the principal NOBILITY, of both Sexes, in England, and declared to be a great natural Curiosity, well worthy the Attention of the Public. She is particularly obliged to the Female Sex who have so liberally patronized her Exhibition, and more especially after the malicious Reports circulated to her Disadvantage after her Arrival in this Kingdom; but which have been long since proved to be groundless. Over her Clothing, which is suitable to this Climate, is worn all the rude Ornaments used by that tribe on Gala Days.

N. B. Elegant Engravings of the Venus, by Lewis, sold at the Room.

ADMITTANCE—ONE SHILLING.

CHESTER, PRINTED BY J. FLETCHER.

Advertisement of Sarah Baartman, the "Hottentot Venus," 1810.

whom P. T. Barnum would eventually market at his American Museum; from patients at the Western Virginia Lunatic Asylum; and from an assortment of distinguished leaders, scholars, and writers, including Napoleon Bonaparte, Dr. Benjamin Rush, James Fenimore Cooper, Noah Webster, Jefferson Davis, and . . . thirteen of the first fourteen presidents of the United States.

Collecting hair samples of this sort, for studying diverse peoples over time, was not merely the passing fancy of quirky naturalists and shameless showmen of centuries long past, as Harvard University had to recently admit. On November 10, 2022, Harvard issued a formal apology for its own massive collection of hair, shorn from seven hundred Native American children, from some three hundred tribal nations, who attended US Indian boarding schools in the 1930s. The hair was collected by Harvard anthropologist George Edward Woodbury and donated to Harvard's Peabody Museum in 1935. "We recognize that for many Native American communities, hair holds cultural and spiritual significance and the Museum is fully committed to the return of hair back to families and tribal communities," its statement read. "The Peabody Museum apologizes to Indigenous families and tribal nations for our complicity in the objectification of Native peoples and for our more than eighty-year possession of hair taken from their relatives."[101] And why did Woodbury collect the hair? "Much of this work was carried out to support, directly or indirectly, scientific racism," admitted the museum. "Descriptions and measurements of hair types were used to justify racial categories and hierarchies."[102] Hair, once again, is seldom simply *hair*.

Hair, once again, is seldom simply hair.

Peter Browne's centuries-old hair specimens have also survived, but only barely, for upon his death in 1860, Browne's albums of hair samples were bequeathed to the Academy of Natural Sciences of Philadelphia (now part of Drexel University), where, in 1976, a curator relegated Browne's collection to the trash bin. Fellow curator Robert McCracken Peck, however, happened upon the "junk," recognized its unusual value, and saved it in his office and later in the academy's archives. He has even attempted to grow the collection since then, by including hair from all living presidents.

In an interview with *National Geographic* in 2018, Peck noted that among the living presidents, George W. Bush had shown little interest in the collection, and Clinton, Obama, and Trump had yet to contribute samples, but Jimmy Carter (39th US president, 1977–81) had been more than accommodating. The affable Georgian, in fact, sent Peck a whole bag of hair clippings, along with a note. "Since returning home from the White House, I have kept [my hair] cut quite short," explained the president, "so these pieces are mostly less than one-half inches long. I did not anticipate growing longer locks for display in a museum!"[103] Should any other living presidents want to contribute their locks to the collection, Peck told me in 2022, "we would be more than happy to add them."[104]

Although few living presidents may be contributing their tresses to museums today, the locks of commanders in chief remain popular with collectors and on the auction circuit. Three strands from the famed pompadour of Ronald Reagan (40th US president, 1981–89), perhaps still slick with the president's go-to product, Brylcreem, were auctioned off for a mere $358.50 in 2006. For about the same price in 2012, one could obtain three silver Yale University–stamped hair and grooming brushes used and owned by the only president who once worked as a male model, Gerald Ford (38th US president, 1974–77)—the auction began at a modest $375.[105]

Much pricier was the 2014 auction of twelve strands from the head of Ulysses S. Grant (18th US president, 1869–77), encased in a gold locket on its original chain; the bidding opened at $8,000. In 2016 a sample hair from Thomas Jefferson (3rd US president, 1801–09) sold for $6,875, though a lock from the snowy mane of Andrew Jackson went for a mere $1,116; the deflated price for the latter's hair perhaps stemmed from an oversaturated market, due

Official portrait of Andrew Jackson, painted by Ralph Eleaser Whiteside Earl, circa 1835.

to the generosity Jackson exhibited to those wanting his locks. On one occasion in 1842, for example, the aging former president allowed some two hundred schoolgirls to snip away at his head to their heart's delight, reportedly procuring "so many of his snow-white locks as to give his head the appearance of having just passed from the hands of the barber."[106]

There were several opportunities for obtaining presidential hair during the 2020 election year, including a single strand from John Adams's (2nd US president, 1797–1801) head that sold for the exacting price of $546.96; a vial of black waves from Richard Nixon (37th US president, 1969–74), which sold for $3,382.50; and a few fine strands from John F. Kennedy's well-cared-for coif went for $1,500. Amazon.com offered free shipping on the Kennedy order and included with the purchase a notarized affidavit from the barber who had snipped the locks from the president's head in July 1963. A bonus item also accompanied the lock of hair from Kennedy's accused assassin that sold at auction in 2017. For a hefty $56,301, the buyer received not only a sizable clump of Lee Harvey Oswald's dark hair, but also . . . the toe tag that identified his corpse. Apparently, one of the ambulance drivers transporting Oswald's body from the morgue to the funeral home just couldn't resist.[107]

In the world of tresses collection and trade, crafty hairstylists and medicos enjoy an inside advantage.

Clearly, in the world of tresses collection and trade, crafty hairstylists and medicos enjoy an inside advantage.

MEMORIALIZING JFK

As this chapter has shown, there are often as many personal reasons as pecuniary and "scholarly" ones for wanting to cut and collect someone's hair, and that was certainly the case in the wake of the assassination of John F. Kennedy on November 22, 1963.

After the president was shot in Dallas at half past noon, he was rushed to nearby Parkland Memorial Hospital, where First Lady Jackie Kennedy handed to the doctors in Trauma Room 1 the parts of her husband's skull that she had collected from the presidential limousine in which her husband had been shot. The doctors worked diligently to save the president's life—with a respirator, blood transfusions, chest compressions, a tracheotomy, a tube down his throat to facilitate breathing—but it was all for naught. The head wound was fatal, and the president was pronounced dead at 1 p.m., less than ninety minutes after the president and First Lady had flown into town.

Forty-eight hours later, nearly to the minute, several of the same doctors who had tried to save Kennedy's life would be busy again, this time across the hall in Trauma Room 2, working feverishly to save the life of another gunshot

President John F. Kennedy and Jacqueline Kennedy arriving at Love Field, Dallas, Texas, on the day of the assassination, by photographer Cecil Stoughton, November 22, 1963.

victim—the person arrested for the president's murder, Lee Harvey Oswald, who had been shot in the basement of the Dallas Police Department while being transferred to the county jail. He had been shot by Mob-tied nightclub owner Jack Ruby in what *Guinness World Records* calls the "first known human killing seen live on TV."[108] Once again, the doctors' efforts were unsuccessful; Oswald died.

After a casket was secured, the president's body was transferred to Air Force One at Dallas's Love Field airport, where Vice President Lyndon Johnson, with First Lady Jackie Kennedy beside him, was sworn in as the next US president. As Johnson took the oath of office, with one hand raised and the other on a Catholic missal (which in the haste of the moment had been mistaken for a Bible), a photographer captured the moment for posterity, showing a dazed Mrs. Kennedy wearing the same raspberry-pink Chanel suit that she had arrived in just a few hours earlier, with one horrifying difference. Like Clara Harris a century earlier, whose hair and clothes were sprayed with blood during the assassination of Lincoln, Mrs. Kennedy, too, was now sodden with the elements of the tragedy that day. Dark splotches adorned her pink suit, white gloves, and stockings from the blood and brain matter that had saturated her while she cradled her mortally wounded husband.

Jackie was asked several times whether she would prefer to change clothes before the photograph was taken, and so she retired to the bathroom. "I saw myself in the mirror," the First Lady recalled. "My whole face was spattered with blood and hair . . . I wiped it off with Kleenex . . . then one second later I thought, why did I wash the blood off? I should have left it there." Although the First Lady washed her face, she adamantly refused to change her outfit. "I want them to see what they've done," she said repeatedly throughout that long and emotional day.[109] As they flew back to Washington, the First Lady sat alongside her husband's flag-draped coffin.

"My whole face was spattered with blood and hair."

The plane landed at Andrews Air Force Base in Maryland that evening, and when Jackie exited the plane with the coffin, observers gasped in horror at the sight of the bloodstained First Lady. The president's body was taken from the plane to Bethesda Naval Hospital for an autopsy and an official recording of the cause of death. At the close of the autopsy, the First Lady and her longtime Secret Service agent, Clint Hill, were asked to enter the examination room for any final questions about the shooting. It was the most difficult moment in the lives of everyone there. The doctor pointed to the right rear of the president's head, where once again hair masked a wound that would change the course of American history. The doctor lifted a flap of the scalp, to which the skin and hair were still attached, revealing "an area in which a good portion of the brain matter is gone," noted Hill. "I close my eyes for a moment, wincing, as the doctor keeps talking."[110]

Johnson Taking Oath, by photographer Cecil W. Stoughton. Image depicts US District Judge Sarah T. Hughes, of the Northern District of Texas, administering the oath of office to Lyndon B. Johnson in the conference room aboard Air Force One at Love Field, Dallas, Texas, on November 22, 1963.

At 4:24 a.m. on Saturday, November 23, the president's body finally arrived back at the White House and was transferred to the East Room, where a hundred years earlier the body of the assassinated Abraham Lincoln had also lain. The family watched in silence, the First Lady still wearing her bloodstained suit, as the coffin was placed on a black catafalque in the center of the room. There it remained until Sunday, when it was transported to the US Capitol to lie in state for public viewing. Prayers were said around the casket, whereupon an exhausted First Lady, now a thirty-four-year-old widow with two young children, finally retired to her private quarters.

At around 12:30 p.m. on Sunday, November 24, just ten minutes after Lee Harvey Oswald had been shot in Dallas and a half hour before the president's casket was scheduled to be transported by a horse-drawn caisson to the US Capitol before a live and global television audience, Hill received a call from General Godfrey McHugh, military aide to the president. "We have a problem," said McHugh—the First Lady wanted to see her husband one final time.[111]

The First Lady wanted to see her husband one final time.

Hill rushed to the first floor of the White House and met up with the general, and upon approaching the entrance to the East Room, they saw Robert "Bobby" Kennedy, the president's brother and the US attorney general, and the First Lady, who had donned a black mourning dress and black-lace veil, peering into the solemn chamber where the president's casket lay. As the four of them entered the room and approached the casket, the military men of the honor guard keeping vigil around the slain president were asked to turn their backs.

After reverently pulling back the flag atop the casket, the general and Hill opened the lid. "When I see President Kennedy lying there, so peaceful," noted Hill, "it's all I can do to keep my emotions in check. Clenching my jaw, I swallow hard." The men then stepped back, giving the First Lady and the president's brother a moment of privacy with the man they so loved.[112]

Standing before the casket, neither Kennedy wanted to let go. Both were crying and beset with grief, and both wanted to remain with the president and stay connected with their lost loved one in some special way. Bobby did so by inserting in his brother's coffin his PT 109 tie clip, a silver rosary, and . . . a lock of his hair. The First Lady, however, was not in the giving mood. As Hill recalled, Jackie suddenly turned to him and asked, "Will you get me a scissor?"

Quickly finding a pair in an office across the hall, Hill rushed back to the East Room, delivered them to Jackie, and then stepped back once again to give her a final, private moment with her husband.[113]

Precious locks of the president's hair would live on with the First Lady.

Snip, snip, snip.

The soft, crisp sound of the scissors is all Hill heard beneath the anguished cries. Precious locks of the president's hair would live on with the First Lady.

John F. Kennedy Lying in State November 25, 1963, by Architect of the Capitol photographers. Image depicts Jacqueline Kennedy and her brothers-in-law, Attorney General Robert Kennedy and Massachusetts Democratic senator Edward "Teddy" Kennedy, as they enter the Capitol rotunda.

Jacqueline Kennedy and Senator Edward "Teddy" Kennedy greet guests during a reception at the White House, following the state funeral of President John F. Kennedy, in the Red Room of the White House, Washington, DC. Photograph by Cecil Stoughton, November 25, 1963.

CHAPTER THREE

POLITICS, DIPLOMACY, AND FAMILY LIFE

HAIR'S MIGHTY IMPACT,

at Home and Abroad

In the summer of 2020, amid a single, seminal seventy-two-hour period, two breaking stories made headlines that altered the trajectory of the presidential election that year—and both stories involved hair. In fact, the only reason these back-to-back stories failed to play an even larger role in the presidential race is that the news cycle surrounding these incidents was interrupted two weeks later by a more consequential political development: the death of Supreme Court Justice Ruth Bader Ginsburg on September 18, which left a highly coveted seat on the high court for President Donald Trump (45th US president, 2017–21) to fill with a conservative justice just weeks before the national election.[114] But the two stories left their mark nonetheless, on Democratic leaders and the Republican president alike—the breaking hair-related stories were equal-opportunity bombshells.

On Monday, August 31, Democratic US Speaker of the House Nancy Pelosi was back home in San Francisco—at a hair appointment.[115] Her stylist had opened the business especially for the Speaker after a Pelosi assistant messaged her. Now, in any normal year, a hair appointment by the Speaker would hardly be newsworthy, but there was nothing normal about 2020. Moreover, politicos always run risks whenever special arrangements are made for them, especially for quotidian tasks like a haircut.

President Bill Clinton (42nd US president, 1993–2001) learned this the hard way in May 1993, when Air Force One sat idle on the tarmac at Los Angeles International Airport, reportedly causing the shutdown of runways and the delay of consumer flights, all so the president could get . . . a haircut—and not just any haircut, but a shearing from an expensive, tony stylist from Beverly Hills.[116] Although fewer flights were actually delayed than initially reported, the incident caused a firestorm with the media, which dubbed it "Hairgate," the "most expensive haircut in history," and the "most famous haircut since Samson's." The president's plane was even christened "Hair Force One," while journalists wondered aloud whether Clinton, a Democrat, could still consider himself a "president of the common man."

The president's plane was even christened "Hair Force One."

Similar musings were aired at French president François Hollande in 2016, amid a scandal dubbed "Coiffeurgate."[117] It seems the French president spent $11,000 a month—$132,000 a year—on trims of his thinly haired pate, a running expense later confirmed by the government; the average French citizen was then earning a mere $41,000 annually. The political optics were horrible for the Socialist leader who called himself "Mr. Normal" and who was elected on a populist platform of attacking the superrich. Not surprisingly, the president's disapproval rating quickly spiked—to 90 percent.

The political optics were horrible for Speaker Pelosi as well, given the setting and timing of her hair appointment—at a salon in San Francisco, during a pandemic, when all city salons had been shuttered by government edict to control the spread of COVID-19. More damaging still, the Speaker's supposed flouting of the law was caught on the salon's security camera, which also showed her not wearing a protective face mask, something she and her party had for months lectured the public on and harangued President Trump for not doing. The Speaker had even requested a blow-dry when indoor blow-drying of hair had also been outlawed, to control the spread of the contagion.

The political optics were horrible for Speaker Pelosi as well, given the setting and timing of her hair appointment—at a salon in San Francisco, during a pandemic, when all city salons had been shuttered by government edict.

Outraged, the salon owner who rented the chair to Pelosi's stylist, an independent contractor—released the security tape to the press. "We have been shut down for so long, not just me, but most of the small businesses," said owner Erica Kious. "I have been fighting for six months for a business that took me twelve years to build to reopen. I am a single mom, I have two small children, and I have no income. We're supposed to look up to this woman, right? It is just disturbing."[118]

The Republicans had a heyday with this story, highlighting what they called Pelosi's arrogant double standard and indifference to the plight of small-business owners suffering under draconian regulations in Democratic-run cities and states. Pelosi fired back, saying she had a different understanding of the civic regulations and had been set up by the owner for political reasons.

Despite her explanation, the episode was embarrassing for the Speaker and her party, especially during a presidential election year.

Donald Trump in the Crosshairs

Three days later, it was President Trump's turn in the cross*hairs* of bad publicity. Jeffrey Goldberg's article in the September 3 edition of *The Atlantic* accused the president of not telling the truth about why he had canceled a visit to the Aisne-Marne American Cemetery and Memorial in Belleau, France, on Saturday, November 10, 2018, to commemorate the hundredth anniversary of the end of World War I.[119]

Trump had blamed the cancellation on "scheduling and logistical difficulties caused by the weather," meaning a cloud ceiling too low for flying the president's helicopter. A last-minute drive to the cemetery was also rejected, due to the traffic disruptions that an impromptu presidential motorcade would doubtless cause in Paris. The cancellation unleashed a barrage of criticism. Winston Churchill's grandson, Nicholas Soames, a Conservative member of the British parliament, was furious, tweeting: "They died with their face to the foe and that pathetic inadequate @realDonaldTrump couldn't even defy the weather to pay his respects to The Fallen." Britain's defense minister Tobias Ellwood agreed, adding "rain did not prevent our brave heroes from doing their job."[120]

But according to Goldberg, writing two years after the event, the controversy was worse than people realized at the time, because that Saturday trip was nixed for reasons other than those indicated by the Trump administration. Citing anonymous sources, Goldberg made the shocking claim that Trump had disparaged the fallen soldiers buried at the cemetery, supposedly telling senior staff members on the morning of the scheduled visit, "Why should I go to that cemetery? It's filled with losers." According to Goldberg, the president had referred to the some 1,800 US Marines who had lost their lives at Belleau Wood as "suckers" for getting killed. If this wasn't appalling enough, Goldberg then followed with this zinger: it wasn't bad weather *per se* that had stopped the president from attending the ceremony; it was the fact that the rain and wind would . . . *mess up his hair.*[121]

Now, there are few characteristics of Donald Trump more discussed and debated, lambasted and lampooned, than his feathery locks. His hair has been the source of endless musings—Is it real?—and horrible puns—a Mane for All Seasons—and late-night host Jimmy Fallon of *The Tonight Show* giggled like a schoolgirl when presented with the opportunity merely to touch and then mess up Trump's famous coif on live TV.[122]

> *There are few characteristics of Donald Trump more discussed and debated, lambasted and lampooned, than his feathery locks.*

Trump is not, of course, the first national leader to be mercilessly mocked for his mane (or for his lack of one). According to the Roman historian Suetonius, Julius Caesar hated his growing baldness so much that he would attempt to cover it by combing his hair forward and by frequently wearing his honorary laurel wreath. His soldiers, who admired Caesar's bravery in battle as well as his prowess with the ladies, mocked him as "our bald whoremonger."[123] Ironically, writers waxed ad nauseum about Trump's hair in the same over-the-top manner that they professed to find so off-putting in the man himself. Trump's hair is "one of the engineering feats of our time," sniggered Dan Fitzpatrick. His "golden coiffure swirls in improbable arches and with an ever-changing consistency—something that Rumpelstiltskin wove during a particularly nasty hangover." Trump's "massive part is no less miraculous than that of Moses in the Red Sea, though who can say whether Trump's version will lead anyone to the Promised Land?" But at the heart of the endless musings about the "coif-in-chief" lingered a belief held by many that "the legendary combover [was] a symbol of his larger-than-life ego and vanity."[124]

To his credit, Trump has made frequent and good-natured references to his carefully maintained appearance. But in the case of *The Atlantic*'s article, the president and his aides who had accompanied him on the trip to Paris vehemently denied the allegations, pointing out that the president had even delivered a memorial speech on Sunday, the day after the Saturday cancellation, and delivered it in the rain and without an umbrella, showing no lack of compassion for the martyred war heroes or special concern for his hair.

Trump's hair is "one of the engineering feats of our time."

Even former national security advisor John Bolton, an ardent Trump detractor who was on the controversial trip to Paris and part of the discussions concerning the Saturday cancellation, also denied the allegations, adding that he would have gladly included this juicy nugget in his recent anti-Trump book had he heard or witnessed the alleged actions by the president. The president (and others) demanded that Goldberg identify his unnamed sources, but to no avail. (Goldberg later admitted that anonymous sources were "not good enough" in reportage at his level, but that he's always "balancing out the moral ambiguities and complications after anonymous sourcing with the public's right to know."[125])

According to Trump's press secretary Kayleigh McEnany, the hair-and-war-memorial contretemps was not only personally devastating to the president

Bronze statue of Julius Caesar, erected in 1936 in *Via dei Fori Imperiali*, and unveiled by Italy's fascist dictator, Benito Mussolini. Sculptor unknown.

but "perhaps the worst" media story of his entire presidency. "What kind of monster would say [the things attributed to him by Goldberg]?" McEnany remembered the president asking. "I know monsters, and even they would not say it," said Trump.[126] Nevertheless, the story stuck with the mainstream media, with the president's many critics, and especially with his Democratic presidential opponent, Joe Biden. And like the Republicans with the Pelosi-in-the-hair-salon incident, they milked it for every ounce of political capital, repeating Goldberg's accusations as verified public fact in debates, interviews, and TV ads.

JOE BIDEN, THE SNIFFER

But not even Trump's successor, Joe Biden (46th US president, 2021–), could escape the political buzz saw caused by hair during that contentious election year. Videos of Biden getting uncomfortably close to women, ostensibly sniffing their hair, became a common meme on social media among Biden detractors, especially during the politically charged period when the #MeToo movement, demanding greater respect for women, was frequently making headlines.

Weirder still, in the eyes of many, was an old video of the former vice president speaking at the dedication of the Joseph R. Biden Jr. Aquatic Center in Wilmington, Delaware, on June 26, 2017, which resurfaced during the campaign and was used and circulated by Trump supporters as further evidence of the septuagenarian's creepiness and age-related incoherence. "I have hairy legs," rambled Biden about his youthful days as a lifeguard, "that turn blonde in the sun. And the kids used to come up and reach in the pool and rub my leg down," and "then watch the hair come back up again." Even liberal media

"Hair Matters," Says Hillary

On May 20, 2001, during her Class Day Address at Yale University, where she had attended law school and met and began dating classmate Bill Clinton, Hillary Clinton, then a former First Lady and current US senator, spoke about her experiences at Yale. She also covered public service, the global AIDS crisis, climate conditions, the challenges facing women, the challenges facing children, and . . . *hair*:

I have to say that in all the years since I've been at Yale, the most important thing that I have to say today is that hair matters. This is a life lesson my family did not teach me, Wellesley or Yale failed to instill in me: the importance of hair. Your hair will send significant messages to those around you. It will tell people who you are and what you stand for. What hopes and dreams you have for the world . . . and especially what hopes and dreams you have for your hair. Likewise, your shoes. But really, more your hair. So, to sum up. Pay attention to your hair. Because everyone else will.[128]

Senator Clinton had learned this lesson early on during her tenure as First Lady. "If I want to knock a story off the front page," she joked, "I just change my hairstyle." And she did, often, throwing red meat to the newshounds hot on her trail for the hidden meaning behind every phase of her "hair-volution," from scrunchie and headband to bouffant and bob. Whatever style she sported, though, one message seemed clear: the hallmark of the Clinton brand would be far from the frills of more glamorous First Ladies such as Jackie Kennedy and Melania Trump. As the London *Guardian* summarized the "Hillary look" during her campaign for the presidency in 2015, it came down to the three Ps: pantsuits, practicality, and power hair.[129]

In each of these incidents from the 2020 presidential race, political damage had been done, and the weapon wielded in every case had been hair.

outlets were disturbed by these incidents. "Why is the former vice president," asked *Esquire*, "telling this story? Does he realize it's making people—like the young girl he puts an arm around at one point—uncomfortable and confused?"[127]

The bottom line: in each of these incidents from the 2020 presidential race, political damage had been done, and the weapon wielded in every case had been hair.

HAIR, FUR, AND DIPLOMACY

If the Trump war-memorial-in-Paris controversy had damaged American foreign policy in 2018, hair—actually, the lack of hair—proved a diplomatic godsend to the United States, in the same Parisian setting, two and a half centuries earlier. In fact, this earlier incident in foreign policy played a pivotal role in saving the American cause during the Revolutionary War, and without the genius of this follicle-challenged Founding Father, there likely would be no institution called the American presidency today.

Now, this Revolutionary leader was not, technically, an American president, though many Americans (21 percent, in fact, according to a 2022 YouGov civics poll) think he was a president.[130] Apparently, some French do as well. "Many French think he was president of the United States," notes Belgian-American biographer Claude-Anne Lopez, and even "the best president you ever had." And who was this clean-domed, president-in-perception-only leader who saved the American cause at a critical time in history? Benjamin Franklin.[131]

Portrait of a wig-wearing Benjamin Franklin seated at a table, reading documents, painted by artist David Martin, 1767. Compare the formality of his attire with the simple brown coat and rustic fur hat that Franklin donned a decade later, as depicted in this chapter's opening illustration.

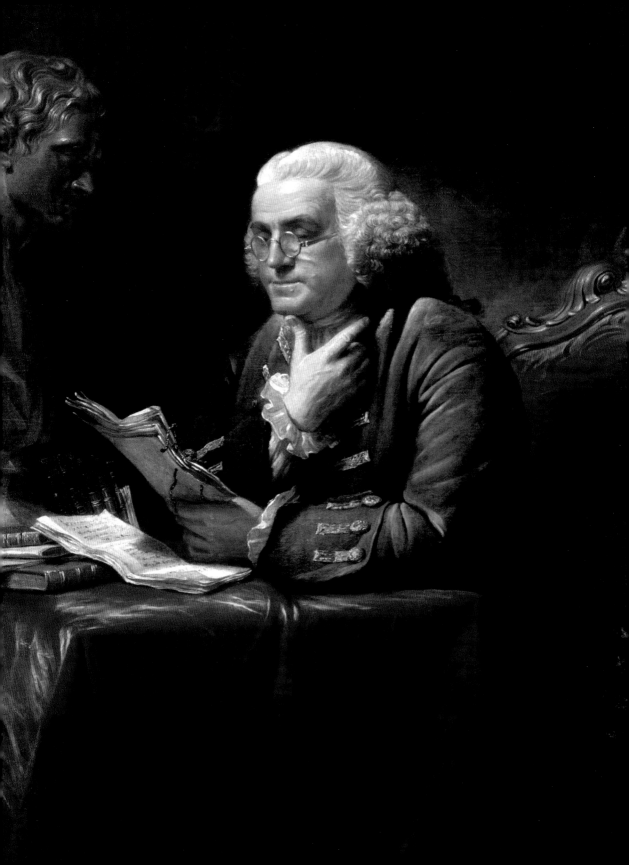

Franklin was the most recognized and honored American of the eighteenth century—and America's best diplomat ever. His many inventions, scientific

> *Franklin was the most recognized and honored American of the eighteenth century—and America's best diplomat ever.*

discoveries, and pathbreaking experiments with electricity had made him a legend in his time, so when the embryonic United States sent him as a special envoy to Paris in 1776 to negotiate a formal alliance with France in support of America's ongoing war for independence against Britain (France's historic enemy), his reputation preceded him.[132]

The city was aglow in his praise, dazzled by the full panoply of his charm, talents, humor, and knowingness—everyone recognized him, and nearly everyone fawned over him. He was seen as that endearing, eccentric savant from the New World, a "noble savage" of sorts, brilliant and self-taught—a walking, talking personification of the Enlightenment. Folks cheered and saluted him whenever he neared, and when he spoke, their necks would crane and ears would bend in rapt fascination for the gem of special insight that his every grunt and utterance was presumed to contain.

Not everyone, however, lapped at the font of this Franklin mania. To the principled but often peevish and envy-ridden John Adams, Franklin was too French, too frivolous, and too frisky with the ladies. He stayed out too late at night and rose too late in the morning for accomplishing a good man's, good day's work. And even once the Good Doctor was finally roused and dressed, the omnipresent army of Franklin fanatics would then descend on him, just "to see the great Franklin," snarled Adams, "and to have the pleasure of telling stories about his simplicity, his balding head and scattering straight hairs."[133]

But what the grudgeful Adams and others could forget at times, amid the frenzy over Franklin, was just how useful this staggering cachet could be to America at this critical time. They "failed to see that Franklin's behavior was part of a stunningly successful—and critical—publicity offensive," wrote historian Thomas Fleming.[134] Stunningly successful, indeed. "My picture is everywhere," noted Franklin in a letter to his daughter, "on the lids of snuff boxes, on rings, busts. The numbers sold are incredible. My portrait is a best seller, you have prints, and copies of prints, and copies of copies spread everywhere. Your father's face is now as well known as the man in the moon."[135]

Basking in adulation was nothing foreign (or unwelcome) to Franklin; he had long worn the mantle of fame, and he relished every moment of it. What was different, however, was his new "celebrity look" that electrified France: that of the unrefined, rustic New World sage. The makeover was stunning—think of a tuxedoed Cary Grant with a slicked-back mane and a martini in hand transformed into a long-haired, barefooted, swilling-from-the-whiskey-bottle Matthew McConaughey. The

transformation to polar opposites was that dramatic, and it was about to pay high dividends for the nascent United States.

"When he first came to France in 1767," notes historian Joanna M. Gohmann, "Franklin wore the clothes of a polite, fashionable Frenchman—a fine European suit and powdered wig—as a way to show respect to the French court."[136] (Fitting Franklin for a wig, by the way, proved no easy feat. When one wigmaker struggled to tug his product down around the diplomat's rather considerable dome,

Portrait of Benjamin Franklin from 1778, oil on canvas by artist Joseph-Siffred Duplessis, circa 1785.

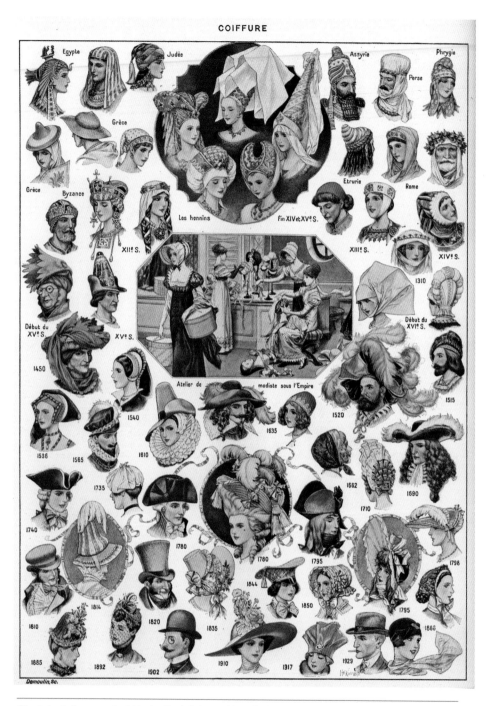

Chart depicting popular historical hairstyles and hair fashion, by Chéri Hérouard, a French illustrator known for his four decades of work with French society magazine *La Vie Parisienne*, circa 1930.

and Franklin ventured to suggest the obvious—that the wig was too small—the peruke master exploded with indignation. Whipping the wig to the floor, he shouted, "No, Monsieur! It is not the wig which is too small; it is your head which is too large!")[137]

But Franklin circumvented all such struggles when he returned to Paris in 1776, for then, notes Gohmann, "he abandoned all the decorum of French dress and instead wore a simple, homespun brown suit, spectacles, and a large fur hat. He cleverly adopted this style as a way to garner attention and appeal to the French for support of the American cause." And clever it was, proving so successful that it provided Franklin with much goodwill to leverage to America's favor, contributing in 1778 to the coveted Treaty of Alliance with France that would seal Britain's defeat in the war in 1781. The conflict officially ended two years later, with the signing of the Treaty of Paris, and one person was critical to winning the support for and negotiating the terms of both historic treaties: Benjamin Franklin.

Key to the "new look" Franklin that took Paris by storm was his fur hat, which he chose over the powdered French wig he had worn the decade before for covering his large, hairless dome. Going wigless in Paris at this time, at least for a dignitary, was an outrageous solecism of statesmanship, a breach of protocol and decorum, and it shocked the silk-clad, wig-wearing, powder-faced aristos of Paris. The French public, however, loved it. Simple and "democratic," the hat became Franklin's trademark. He wore it everywhere, even indoors, which was yet another well-calculated *faux pas* by Franklin the fox that only drew further attention to himself.

In fact, it wasn't long before the hat, along with his whole rustic garb and getup, became seen as a symbol of America itself and synonymous with the American cause—which is exactly the effect Franklin had hoped to induce—reflecting the country's innocence, simplicity, and humble beginnings; its bucolic charm and untamed frontier; and its bold and exciting experiment in freedom from a corrupted and corrupting Old World empire, England.

A police report made on Franklin right after his arrival in Paris took special

THE POLITICS OF
THE MULLET

In the parlance of pop culture, Franklin's hairstyle during his fur-hat days was a "skullet" (bald on the top and long hair in the back), which itself is a form of the much-mocked "mullet," aka the "bi-level," the "Kentucky waterfall," "hockey hair," or "business up front and a party in the back." In Franklin's case, the long hair that peeked out from beneath his fur hat was a radical look, one that worked to America's favor during the Revolutionary War, as this chapter has shown. "Think how this must appear among the powder'd heads of Paris!" Franklin mused.[139]

Franklin was not, however, the only "US president" to turn heads with his "party in the back" hairstyle. A half century after him and more than a century before mullets became popular in the 1980s, President James Polk (11th US president, 1845–49) sported an outstanding one. His long, straight, graying-brown hair, cut short on the sides and top and combed straight back, trailed several inches beneath his ears and collar, resulting in a neat and masterful rendition of the style that remains the envy of mullet lovers today.

But there's a more recent mullet master among the presidential class, one nearly always forgotten, given the historic photos popularly associated with him—and that's unfortunate, because there are political insights to be gleaned from these tresses that trailed behind him. When one thinks of Lyndon Baines Johnson (36th US president, 1963–69), one commonly envisions his White House days of the 1960s, when he first served as vice president under John F. Kennedy and then as president after Kennedy was killed. Ingrained in public memory is the famed photo of him, on a crowded Air Force One, taking the presidential oath of office just hours after Kennedy's assassination on November 22, 1963. His thinning hair is cut short and conservatively combed back—a style simple, clean, and conventional, worn by nearly every other man seen standing alongside LBJ in that historic shot.

The Johnson most folks never remember, however, is the LBJ of 1972–73, right before he died, when he had retired from public life to his ranch in Texas, having long lost the support of the country and his party for a second term in office due to the mess in Vietnam, which only worsened during his presidency. This later Johnson was—in a word—hip, which is the ultimate irony, considering it was long-haired hippies and anti–Vietnam War protesters who had led the charge against his reelection campaign in 1968 with such chants as, "Hey, hey, LBJ! How many kids did you kill today?" His long gray hair, upon his death in January 1973, was nearly shoulder-length, shocking the public who hadn't seen a picture of him in years.

Many wondered about the reason for the long locks, especially on someone whose career had been decimated by long-haired bohemians. A July 1973 article in *The Atlantic Monthly* by Leo Janos, published shortly after Johnson's death, perhaps provides the key to unlocking the irony:

The newspapers showed a startling picture of Johnson, his hair almost shoulder-length. Former aide Bob Hardesty takes credit for this development. "We were working together one day," Hardesty recalls, "and he [Johnson] said, in passing, 'Robert, you need a haircut.' I told him, 'Mr. President, I'm letting my hair grow so no one will be able to mistake me for those SOB's in the White House.' He looked startled, so I explained, 'You know, that bunch around Nixon—Haldeman, Ehrlichman—they all have very short hair.' He nodded. The next time I saw him his hair was growing over his collar."[140]

If this explanation is correct, then LBJ grew his hair long, consciously or not, as a protest against the buzz-cut Republican "yes-men" of the Nixon administration who succeeded him in office—men whose haircuts emulated those of the young draftees they sent to war, and men who would soon embroil the country in a Vietnam on the home front, in a quagmire called Watergate.

Former US president Lyndon B. Johnson with long hair, pictured meeting with John McCormack and Tommy Corcoran at the LBJ Ranch near Stonewall, Texas. Photograph by Frank Wolfe, August 19, 1972.

note of his hair, hat, and celebrityhood. "Doctor Franklin, who lately arrived in this country from the English colonies, is very much run after, and feted," it read. "He has an agreeable physiognomy. Spectacles always on his eyes, but little hair—a fur cap is always on his head. He wears no powder, but a neat air. Linen very white [and] a brown coat makes his dress. His only defense is a stick in his hand."[138]

Franklin's hat even spurred a Parisian hairstyling craze, as ladies so adored Franklin and his piquant charms (and he gladly adored their piquant charms in return, in every imaginable way) that they began wearing custom wigs designed specifically to resemble his famous fur hat. Called the coiffure à la Franklin, it is arguably the most politically consequential hairstyle in history.

Franklin's hat even spurred a Parisian hairstyling craze, as ladies so adored Franklin and his piquant charms . . . that they began wearing custom wigs designed specifically to resemble his famous fur hat.

THE LONG-HAIR LOVE OF HARRY AND BESS TRUMAN

Long hair was also a key factor in one of the great, underappreciated love stories in American history, that of Bess and Harry Truman (33rd US president, 1945–53). Now, Truman had a wonderful eye for style, and after returning a hero from World War I, he and a buddy opened a haberdashery in Kansas City, Missouri, selling menswear and accessories. In fact, throughout his political life, Truman was known for his dapper appearance and meticulously fitted, bespoke suits (almost always double-breasted with the requisite pocket square). In fact, until his ascension to the presidency in 1945 upon the death of Franklin Roosevelt (32nd US president, 1933–45), many citizens hardly knew him for anything else.

Roosevelt, as he privately made clear, hadn't wanted Truman as his vice president, but the party had balked at keeping Henry Wallace as VP, given Wallace's Soviet sympathies, so Truman was selected as his replacement. Roosevelt, however, snubbed his new vice president, seldom ever meeting face-to-face with the haberdasher from Missouri who suddenly, upon the president's death on April 12, became the most powerful man in the world, soon armed with the atomic bomb. "Is there anything I can do for you?" asked Truman of Eleanor Roosevelt, upon learning of her husband's death. "Is there anything we can do for *you*?" replied the First Lady. "For you are the one in trouble now."[141]

So perhaps it's not surprising, given Truman's fastidious style and sartorial acumen, that the first thing the future president noticed about his future wife was her appearance.

So perhaps it's not surprising, given Truman's fastidious style and sartorial acumen, that the first thing the future president noticed about his future wife was her appearance. The two had been Sunday school classmates in Independence, Missouri, in 1890, and what specifically had captivated six-year-old Harry about five-year-old Bess was . . . her gorgeous hair. In fact, it was love at first sight. "I saw a beautiful curly haired girl," remembered the president. "I thought (and still think) she was the most beautiful girl I ever saw. She had tanned skin, blond hair, golden as sunshine, and the most beautiful eyes I've ever seen or ever will see."[142]

The two attended school together from fifth grade through graduation from high school in 1901, when Harry moved outside of town to work on a family farm. Harry pursued Bess for the next two decades, and after his battlefront service in France in World War I, they finally wed in 1919. No couple was more committed and faithful to each other. When an army officer at the Potsdam Conference in

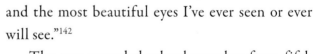

Photograph of Bess Truman at about age four-and-a-half, photographer unknown, circa 1889.

Germany in late July and early August 1945—where Truman met with UK prime minister Winston Churchill and Soviet premier Joseph Stalin to discuss Germany's defeat and the immediate fate and future of postwar Europe—assured Truman that he could "arrange anything you like while you're here—anything in the way of wine and women," the president lashed out with indignation. "I married my sweetheart," he upbraided the officer. "She doesn't run around on me and I don't run around on her. . . . Don't ever mention that kind of stuff to me again."[143]

Evidence of Truman's abiding love for his wife is the epistolary treasure of some 1,300 letters he wrote to her. Buried amid the missives is a topic that became a point of contention for the couple in the summer of 1925. The subject? Bess's long hair. While Harry was off training with his army reserve unit, Bess got the itch to do something radical: cut her hair, trading in her long locks for the short and sleek bob made famous by the Jazz Age flappers of the then "Roaring Twenties."

While Harry was off training with his army reserve unit, Bess got the itch to do something radical: cut her hair.

The new hairstyle was simple and chic, and though Bess was forty years old, she still wanted in on the fad (especially during the drippy days of summer in Missouri, before air-conditioning was common and when wearing long hair was hot and uncomfortable). Harry, however, had been in love with Bess's "golden curls" since childhood, and she in turn loved Harry too much to do anything rash, even cutting her hair, if it meant upsetting him. Thus began an endearing correspondence about hair and haircuts—and mutual love and respect—between a future president and a future First Lady.

Photograph of President Harry S. Truman and Mrs. Bess Truman on the porch of their Independence, Missouri, home, 1953.

Tammy Williams, archivist and social media coordinator at the Harry S. Truman Presidential Library and Museum, has done a wonderful job of ordering this loving correspondence over locks.[144] Bess begins the exchanges with a time-honored strategy used by wives throughout history—she first tries to soften up her husband, bringing him around slowly to her point of view. She informs him, in a July 7 letter, that his own cousin Nellie, who lived across the street from them, "has had her hair cut and she looks perfectly fine." Moreover, she adds, "Ethel [Nellie's sister] is going to do it this week." But Bess is too excited to pussyfoot around for long—she "cuts" quickly to the cut:

> I am crazier than ever to get mine off—Why won't you agree enthusiastically? My hair grows so fast, I could soon put it up again if it looked very badly—Please!—I'm much more conspicuous having long hair than I will be with it short.

Before Harry even had time to reply, another letter from Bess arrived the following day, July 8:

> Ethel had her hair cut today and she looks great. When may I do it? I never wanted to do anything as badly in my life. Come on, be a sport. Ask all the married men in camp about their wives' heads & I'll bet anything I have there isn't one under sixty who has long hair.

The future president replied promptly, on July 9, explaining in plain terms that what mattered to him was not the length of her hair but her happiness:

> Say, if you want your hair bobbed so badly, go on and get it done. I want you to be happy regardless of what I think about it. I am very sure you'll be just as beautiful with it off and I'll not say anything to make you sorry for doing it. I can still see you as the finest on earth so go and have it done. I've never been right sure you weren't kidding me anyway. You usually do as you like about things and that's what I want you to do.

Bess was so moved by Harry's letter that she almost refused to go through with the haircut, replying to Harry on July 12:

> That was a dear letter you wrote me about bobbing my hair—it almost put a crimp in my wanting to do it. But if you knew the utter discomfort of all this pile on top of my head—and the time I waste every day getting it there you would insist upon me cutting it. I most sincerely hope you'll never feel otherwise than you said you do in that letter—for life would be a dreary outlook if you ever ceased to feel just that way.

The future First Lady thus cut her tresses, keeping her hair short for the remainder of her life. When Harry died in 1972, he had coexisted with his wife's short coif for nearly a half century—and never, as far as anyone can tell, had he ever loved Bess one strand less than the first time he laid eyes on that "beautiful curly haired girl" eighty-two years before.

HAIR, LOVE, WAR, AND THE GRANTS

Hair, love, and war were at the heart of another endearing presidential relationship, that of President Ulysses S. Grant and his wife, Julia. Upon graduation from West Point in 1843, the twenty-one-year-old second lieutenant made his way to St. Louis, where he reported for duty with the army's regiment at nearby Jefferson Barracks, Missouri. Also nearby was the home of his West Point roommate, Frederick T. Dent, who invited Grant to visit his

First Lady Bess Truman, circa 1944–53.

family's modest slave-run plantation. Grant soon became a fixture at the Dents' Sunday dinners, and it was on these occasions, in February 1844, that Grant first met Frederick's eighteen-year-old sister, Julia, who had just graduated and returned from her boarding school in St. Louis.

Julia was not attractive—she was cross-eyed, no less, which is why nearly every photo of her was taken from the side, instead of from the front, to hide her affliction—and she was not known for her sterling intellect. But she had a warm, fun-loving personality that the reserved and soft-spoken Grant found endearing, and the attraction between the two was mutual and immediate. Grant soon began visiting the estate regularly, just to see her. They rode horses together and read poetry to each other, and there seemed to be nothing that Grant wouldn't do for the new love of his life. "At one point her pet canary died," notes historian and biographer Gilbert King, "and Grant crafted a small yellow coffin and summoned eight fellow officers for an avian funeral service."[145]

But within months, their courtship was interrupted by pending war. Grant was sent to the front lines in Mexico (serving under future US president Zachary Taylor), where tensions were brewing over the territory of Texas, which would soon spill over into the Mexican-American War of 1846–48. Before separating, they sealed their commitment to each other with special

Rare frontal photograph of Julia Dent Grant, depicting her strabismus (cross-eyedness), shown with her eldest children, Frederick Dent Grant and Ulysses S. Grant Jr., photographer unknown, 1854.

gifts: Grant gave Julia his West Point ring, and in return he received a snippet of her hair, which he encased in a locket and wore on a silver chain around his neck.[146]

Grant would not return for four years, though when he did, he and Julia finally wed, in 1848. They would have four children. But long, lonely periods of separation followed, as is customary with careers in the military, periods that Grant found nearly unbearable. To survive them, he relied on two coping methods. First, he became a scripturient-soldier, an inveterate letter writer, penning hundreds of love letters to his wife, messages often written within earshot and bloodshed of the battlefield and nestled with flower petals and locks of his hair.[147] His second method of coping was potentially more destructive: drinking. Grant could indeed be a heavy drinker, though he was not the noxious drunkard some of his jealous critics and political opponents made him out to be.[148]

But cope he did, and he and Julia survived through frequent and daunting peaks and valleys—from his victory as the "Hero of Appomattox" in the Civil War and their two terms in the White House, with all the fame and adulation that accompanies becoming a president and a First Lady, to extraordinary periods of financial boom and bust; yet, through it all, they remained true to each other to the very end.

Despite his hairy, beard-gruff appearance and tenacity in battle, Grant was, at heart, a gentle and romantic soul, as his trove of love letters to Julia bears out. His tender side was on full display in the sensitive way he handled a touchy issue for Julia—her strabismus

Julia was not attractive—she was cross-eyed, no less, which is why nearly every photo of her was taken from the side, instead of from the front, to hide her affliction—and she was not known for her sterling intellect.

(cross-eyedness). After Grant had been elected president, Julia considered a highly risky eye surgery to correct her condition, so as not to be such an "embarrassment" to her husband. "Why, you are getting to be such a great man," she told him, "and I am such a plain little wife. I thought if my eyes were as others are I might not be so very, very plain." Grant would have none of that, replying with such grace, affection, compassion, and sensitivity that Julia could never doubt his heartfelt love for her. "Did I not see you and fall in love with you with these same eyes?" he asked. "I like them just as they are, and now, remember, you are not to interfere with them. They are mine, and let me tell you, Mrs. Grant, you had better not make any experiments, as I might not like you half so well with any other eyes."[149]

This touching display of devotion, however, was not so moving that it blinded one of the undertakers to a prime opportunity.

This tender side to the president was evident to the day he died, as his undertakers discovered upon Grant's death from throat and tongue cancer, due to his incurable cigar habit, on July 23, 1885, at the age of sixty-three. For upon undressing the president, to prepare his body for his funeral, they discovered something special: residing on Grant's chest, right next to his heart, was the silver chain with the locket containing something dear—Julia's hair, which she had given to Grant some forty years before.

President Ulysses S. Grant, photographed by Matthew Brady, circa 1870s.

General Grant and his family, photographer unknown, 1868.

This touching display of devotion, however, was not so moving that it blinded one of the undertakers to a prime opportunity. For as presidential barbers and undertakers have done throughout history, he took the occasion of his proximity to fame to gather a few mementos of the moment: he trimmed and saved snippets of the president's hair and samples of his beard, enclosing them in a gold locket with a picture of Grant. He even presciently signed and dated a note proving the provenance of the trimmings, useful in any future sale of the famous locks. When the hair was auctioned in 2014, the minimum bid was a respectable $8,000.[150]

THE LOCKS, LOVE, AND LOSS OF "SILENT CAL"

Hair, humor, and tragedy were all components of yet another successful, long-lasting presidential marriage, that of Grace and Calvin Coolidge (30th US president, 1923–29). Their relationship was proof in excelsis that opposites attract. Whereas Grace was a warm and vibrant, pleasantly plump, gregarious lass with beautiful olive skin and an infectious smile ("Sunshine" was the Secret Service's nickname for the First Lady), Calvin was a prim-lipped, pinch-faced scarecrow of a man incongruously devoted to discipline and frugality during a Jazz Age decade of wild excess and extraordinary national growth, a man with little need for either the cadre of friends or vociferous social life that Grace so enjoyed.

In fact, in contrast to Grace's *joie de vivre*, shy "Silent Cal," as he was dubbed, seemed allergic to conversation, laughter, and levity, and he suffered from so many respiratory and digestive ailments that he was forever coughing, popping pills, and inhaling nasal sprays. Not surprisingly, this little stoat of a man was the brunt of endless jokes, in his lifetime and after. Alice Roosevelt Longworth, the acid-tongued eldest child of Theodore Roosevelt, said Coolidge looked as though he had been "weaned

Not surprisingly, this little stoat of a man was the brunt of endless jokes, in his lifetime and after.

on a pickle," and when informed in 1933 that Coolidge had died, the literary dynamo Dorothy Parker wondered how they could tell—he always looked that way.

In fact, other than their New England backgrounds—a common birth in Vermont and advanced schooling in Massachusetts—Grace and Calvin had virtually nothing in common. But strangely, somehow, this oddest of odd couples shared a sweet synergy and complemented each other, and the hilarity of their obvious differences drew them together, cementing their relationship and making them a popular duo on the DC social scene. (A notorious penny-pincher,

President Calvin Coolidge and First Lady Grace Coolidge outside the White House, by photographers Harris & Ewing, November 5, 1924.

Coolidge would gladly accept invitations to free dinners. "Gotta eat somewhere," he'd say.)

Calvin's success was also attractive to Grace, though he was successful in a painfully plodding way befitting his anything-but-flashy demeanor. For example, after graduating from Amherst College in Massachusetts in 1895 and then passing the bar and beginning his law practice in nearby Northampton two years later, there was seemingly no political office too minor or middling that this low-profile Republican wouldn't hold while quarter-inching his way up the political ladder. He began as a city councilman, followed by city solicitor, county clerk, local chairman of the Republican Party, state legislator, Northampton mayor, state senator, state senate president, lieutenant governor, governor of Massachusetts, Republican candidate for the presidency, vice president of the United States under Warren Harding (29th US president, 1921–23), and, upon Harding's death from a heart attack on August 2, 1923, finally president of the United States.[151] It was an "improbable" ascent,

President Calvin Coolidge, May 9, 1924.

notes biographer Amity Shlaes, one full of "near failure," but "at every stage, Coolidge did push forward, and so triumph."[152] He was a paragon of perseverance.

But there was another quality about Calvin that Grace—and others—found endearing: his deadpan style of wit and humor. This quality may sound surprising, considering Coolidge's taciturn ways and reputation as a snore of a man, but when he did talk, he was often entertaining, noted for memorable quips and wry offhand sallies. A wonderful example of this is the famed tale of the DC hostess hell-bent on engaging Coolidge in conversation. "You must talk to me, Mr. Coolidge," she said to the vice president. "I made a bet today that I could get more than two words out of you." "You lose," quipped Coolidge.

Calvin and Grace's first meeting was even laden with humor—and a factor of hair. The year was 1904, and they lived across the street from each other in Northampton, where Calvin was a busy lawyer, working his way through the ranks of local politics, and Grace was teaching nearby at the Clarke Institute for the Deaf. One morning, while outside watering flowers, Grace caught sight of Calvin through an open window in his boardinghouse. He was wearing long underwear while shaving in a mirror, with a derby hat balanced on the back of his head—the hat, he later explained, was for holding his uncombed hair out of his eyes while shaving.[153] (Years later in the White House, Coolidge discovered yet another way to keep his unruly morning mane out of his eyes: while lolling abed eating breakfast, he had a White House attendant massage his hair and scalp with Vaseline, which was then popularly hailed as a miracle drug of sorts with assorted healing powers.)

Calvin and Grace's first meeting was even laden with humor—and a factor of hair.

Upon seeing the ridiculous-looking beanpole of a man in the window, Grace burst out laughing, guffawing so loudly that the well-lathered Calvin, razor in hand, turned and noticed the dark-haired beauty below. Soon after this incident, she delivered, via the janitor from her dormitory (who conveniently worked in Calvin's building too), a potted flower to the skinny little shaver in the window, and the janitor returned with Calvin's calling card. A relationship blossomed; they wed in 1905.

Calvin's rise to political prominence and the White House followed over the next two decades, along with the birth of two boys, John and Calvin, Jr., and it was the 1924 tragedy tied to the latter son, with whom the president was especially close, that forever changed Coolidge and his presidency—if not also the country.

The pivotal day was June 30, when the president had gathered Grace and the boys at the White House for a family photo. John, age seventeen, and Calvin, Jr., sixteen, were home from school, and after the photo was taken, the boys rushed to shed their suits in the summer heat and hit the White House courts for an intense, intersibling tennis match. After several hard-fought games, one of Calvin's feet began to ache, causing a cancellation of the

Calvin, Jr. stands on the left in a photograph of the Coolidge family taken on June 30, 1924, the fateful day when he got a blister on his toe playing tennis with his brother John (standing on the right). His toe became infected and led to his death one week later. Photographer unknown.

fun. The boys returned to the White House, whereupon Calvin removed his sneakers and found a blister on the top of the third toe of his right foot. It seems, in his haste to hit the courts, Calvin had failed to put socks on when changing into his sneakers, and the heavy friction that resulted during his sockless play had caused the sore.

Within days of the tennis match, Calvin was limping and running a fever. His glands then swelled, the blister darkened, and red lines began streaking his legs. Tragically, the blister had become infected, and the infection had now entered the boy's bloodstream. Young Calvin was soon in horrible pain, delirious from a peaking fever, begging his father for help. Desperate to do something, to do anything to help his son, the president at one point even ran onto the White House lawn and caught a brown bunny, bringing it back for Calvin, who loved animals, to help divert his son's attention from his mounting agony.[154]

With his situation worsening, Calvin was transferred to Walter Reed Army Medical Center, one of the best hospitals of the day. But the doctors were helpless; Alexander Fleming's discovery of that antibacterial wonder drug called penicillin was still four years away. Frustrated and scared, the president could do nothing for his son but sit by his side, listen to his screams, and pray that the pain would soon pass. But it wouldn't. When Calvin began struggling to breathe, he was put on oxygen, but a wrong valve was opened on the auxiliary tank, and it exploded, injuring one of Calvin's doctors.

Clearly, the situation was growing from horrible to worse, when a doctor finally informed the president that his son was nearing death. "The President sprang from his chair," the doctor noted, "and took his dying son in his arms, shouting hysterically into his ears that he would soon join him in the great beyond, and requesting that young Calvin so inform his grandmother," the president's mother.[155]

To calm himself and soothe his son, the president

To calm himself and soothe his son, the president then pulled from his pocket one of his most prized possessions—a gold locket containing a snippet of his mother's hair.

then pulled from his pocket one of his most prized possessions—a gold locket containing a snippet of his mother's hair, a keepsake preserved from her deathbed—and then pressed it into young Calvin's hand. Too weak to hold it, Calvin dropped the locket several times, and each time the president retrieved it and returned it to his son's grasp, as if to reassure him that he would not be alone in heaven. At 10:20 p.m. on July 7, while the president held his son—with one hand on his son's hand, with the precious locket in their grasp, and the other gently stroking his son's forehead and hair—young Calvin died. Only a week had passed since that happy family photo at the White House and that fateful day of tennis.[156]

The president, formerly so famous for his icy stoicism and imperturbability, morphed quickly into a man no one had ever seen. Grief unhinged him; he became an emotional wreck. "He was not the president of the United States," noted reporter John Lambert. "He was the father, overcome by grief and love for his boy. He wept unafraid, unashamed." The president was, in a word, inconsolable. "It is commonly stated that President Coolidge is 'cold as ice,'" noted John Albert Kolmer, one of the doctors who had tended to Calvin, "but I had the opportunity of seeing him in his hour of grief and to know quite otherwise. Indeed, it was the most touching and heart-rending experience of my whole professional career."[157]

"He was not the president of the United States. He was the father, overcome by grief and love for his boy."

Calvin's body was returned to the White House, where it lay in state in the East Room. Late at night, White House staff would find the president in his nightshirt, aside his son's casket, softly stroking his son's head and hair, adrift in grief. (Lincoln had done the same with the dead body of his son Willie.)

Coolidge would never fully recover from the ordeal, and the tragedy affected his remaining years in office. "Coolidge himself struggled with a clinical depression that made inactivity and passivity the principal features of his Administration," writes historian Robert Dallek. He became "saddled with a host of depressive symptoms," adds Joshua Kendall in *First Dads: Parenting and Politics from George Washington to Barack Obama* (2016), "including a low energy level, a lack of interest in daily activities, hypersomnia, digestive problems, and feelings of hopelessness and helplessness."[158]

So, as the country barreled toward an economic depression that would cripple the country, mirroring the emotional depression arguably crippling the president, the despondent Coolidge appeared to some, then and today, "asleep at the switch." From this perspective, the detached and depressed Coolidge, through what William Allen White called the president's "masterly inactivity for which he was so splendidly equipped," had failed to tame or temper the financial buccaneering and corporate thimblerigging lead-ing the country to that national hangover called the Great Depression. The fairness of this assessment, or whether it smacks of more post hoc, ergo propter hoc—more Monday-morning quarterbacking, with the brilliant assistance of hindsight—than sound historical analysis, has long been debated, and Coolidge has his defenders. But what is cer-tainly true is that Coolidge increasingly lost interest in the presidency in the wake of his son's death, and he chose not to run for reelection in 1928.

"When [Calvin] went," admitted Coolidge, "the power and glory of the presidency went with him."[159]

"When [Calvin] went . . . the power and glory of the presidency went with him."

CHAPTER FOUR

HAIR, IMAGE, AND INFIDELITIES

THE CASE OF

John F. Kennedy

For many Americans, the power and glory of the presidency left with the passing of a later president, John F. Kennedy. It's a cliché but true that individuals old enough to remember that tragic day in Dallas on November 22, 1963, when President Kennedy was shot, can recall exactly where they were and exactly what they were doing, when they heard the flashing news that the president had been killed.

Kennedy's youthfulness, idealism, style, and eloquence had galvanized

But such fleshment spilled over into outright obsession in the weeks and months after Kennedy took office in January 1961.

the country like few presidents ever had, making him a touchstone of a generation and inspiring legions of youth toward greater selflessness, political engagement, and service to humanity. From the formation of the Peace Corps, a commitment to civil rights, and a concern for social justice to the seemingly ludicrous notion that even extraterrestrial bodies such as the Moon lay within the reach of American ingenuity—Kennedy's thousand days in the White House had inspired all this, which is why his shocking death in such a shocking manner hit the country, and the world, so very hard.

This dizzying adoration of the president (and of his glamorous wife, Jackie) was evident from the very start of his campaign for the presidency. But such

John, Jackie, and Caroline Kennedy, photographed by Jacques Lowe, 1960.

fleshment spilled over into outright obsession in the weeks and months after Kennedy took office in January 1961, when the world and the world's media couldn't get enough of the dynamic new king and queen of America's "Camelot," as their brief time in the White House would later be christened (at Jackie's insistence).

From what John and Jackie wore to what they ate, the world wanted to know—including what the dazzling new American president read. When Kennedy, in a March 1961 article in *LIFE* magazine, listed among his ten favorite books Ian Fleming's *From Russia, with Love* (1957), the fifth of Fleming's James

Bond novels, the effect of the endorsement was stunning and swift: Fleming suddenly became the bestselling spy novelist in the world, selling millions of copies of his books and spawning the phenomenal film franchise that continues to this day.

JAMES BOND IN THE WHITE HOUSE

One might think that the upper-crust Kennedy would have been too highbrow and cultured to like Fleming's brand of pulp fiction. After all, Kennedy had already authored two bestselling books, *Why England Slept* (1940), at the age of twenty-three, and *Profiles in Courage* (1956), for which he received the Pulitzer Prize. But appearances can be deceiving, and they always were in the case of Kennedy.

Actually, there were numerous similarities among the fictional secret agent, his creator, and the new president. All enjoyed wealth and elite educations (Bond and Fleming went to Eton; Kennedy to Harvard). All exuded an overt machismo and were dashing and dapper—from manicured hair to polished shoes—seemingly born to wear a tux or tailored suit. All had a boyish zeal for action (Bond and Fleming dabbled in everything from gambling and fast cars to spelunking and shark hunting, while Kennedy's fondness for sailing and his family's raucous games of football at their compound at Hyannis Port mesmerized the world's media). Derring-do marked each man's experience in World War II (Fleming, like Bond, wore the rank of a naval commander and survived dangerous bombings and operations, while Kennedy's harrowing PT-109 incident made him a legend). And all three men became famous Cold War warriors.

Showing affinity for a character like Bond

and the heavily eroticized Bond phenomenon was certainly not out of character for Kennedy. In fact, an association with Bond only further solidified the perception of the president as an active, athletic, healthy man of action—a man's man, someone decisive, tough, confident, dependable, and successful. This Kennedy tie to Bond remained strong until nearly the day he died, as exemplified by the *New Yorker* cartoon published just months before the president was slain. The cartoon depicted the White House late at night, with a light still on; the ever-dedicated Kennedy was ostensibly still awake and hard at work managing yet another global crisis on behalf of the American people. "Then again," read the caption, "it may merely be the new Ian Fleming [book]."[160]

So, when Kennedy had the opportunity to dine with Fleming at the Kennedys' home in Georgetown on March 13, 1960, eight months before his election to the presidency, the Massachusetts senator jumped at the

President Kennedy and his brothers, Attorney General Robert F. Kennedy and Senator Edward "Teddy" Kennedy, at the White House, outside the Oval Office. Photographed by Cecil W. Stoughton, August 28, 1963.

opportunity. Fleming was in Washington for a newspaper interview, and while driving around Georgetown with an old friend—socialite Marion "Oatsie" Leiter (whose surname was co-opted by Fleming for his character of Felix Leiter, the CIA operative and longtime Bond friend)—they happened upon Jack and Jackie strolling along the sidewalk. The meeting was fortuitous, for Leiter was to dine at the Kennedys' home that evening. She promptly pulled her car over and introduced the celebrities. "James Bond?" said Kennedy, upon seeing Fleming. (According to Fleming's more flattering rendition of the story, Kennedy said instead, "*the* Ian Fleming?"[161]) Jack and Jackie gladly invited the famed writer to join them for dinner—a dinner, surprisingly, that would pivot on hair.

Jack and Jackie gladly invited the famed writer to join them for dinner—a dinner, surprisingly, that would pivot on hair.

During the postmeal coffee, the Cold War became the focus of discussion, and how the United States should deal with Cuba's new Communist leader, Fidel Castro. From Fleming's perspective, America didn't need to "eliminate" the dictator, just humiliate him, and the key to doing this, he suggested, was hair—in particular, facial hair.

Fleming then outlined a seemingly ludicrous plot for dropping leaflets over Cuba, informing its citizens that the beards so popularly worn by its revolutionary leadership class were magnets for attracting radioactivity from nearby atomic bomb tests by the United States, and that the trapped radioactivity would cause impotence. Cuba's leaders, it was believed, would likely either shave off their beards or face humiliation by showing their vulnerability and powerlessness.

Fleming biographer Andrew Lycett says the writer floated the notion "with his tongue firmly in his cheek."[162] But Fleming had outlined and enacted equally absurd-sounding counterintelligence actions against the Nazis during World War II, and some of them had been wildly successful (such as "Operation Mincemeat," which involved dressing the dead body of a London vagrant, who had killed himself with rat poison, in the uniform of a British serviceman, filling his pockets with bogus war plans, and then floating his corpse off the coast of Spain for German agents to find; the plan worked to perfection). Kennedy, ever charming, smiled with amusement at the writer's seemingly outrageous idea, though the next day the director of the CIA himself, Allen Dulles (who had been given a copy of Fleming's *From Russia, with Love* by none other than Jackie Kennedy, who noted, "Here is a book you should have, Mr. Director"), attempted to track down Fleming to speak with him, but the writer had already left for the airport.

Unbeknownst to Fleming, the CIA began planning the Bay of Pigs invasion of Cuba that very month, and the following year, in late 1961, the Kennedy administration launched "Operation Mongoose," a covert plan to overthrow the Cuban Communist regime. Assorted bizarre plans for killing Castro had been fashioned just prior to and during this operation, from poisoning his pens, pills, speeches, wet suit, and even milkshakes to funneling him explosive shellfish and cigars. One idea, revealed in a 1975 US Senate Intelligence Committee report, was to apply highly toxic thallium salt to Castro's cigars or shoes.[163] Thallium was then commonly used in rat poisons and ant killers, and it had one major effect on humans contaminated with the chemical—hair loss.

It seems Fleming's dinner with Kennedy was more consequential than the writer realized.

This would cause, hoped the CIA, Castro's "beard, eyebrows, and pubic hair to fall out," embarrassing the leader. The CIA, in fact, was reportedly on the verge of executing the scheme when a sudden change in the Cuban leader's travel plans undercut the opportunity. It seems Fleming's dinner with Kennedy was perhaps more consequential than the writer realized.

In fact, the Kennedy administration's obsession with Bond knew few bounds. According to Dulles biographer Stephen Kinzer, CIA technicians were even instructed to replicate 007's special gadgetry, such as his secret homing devices. To Kinzer, Kennedy and Dulles "conflated reality with the Bond novels," which ultimately "strengthened their faith in covert action. It was a case of life imitating art imitating life, as when gangsters watch gangster movies for tips on how they should behave."[164]

KENNEDY—THE MAN, THE MYTH

Also likely unknown to Fleming was how seriously Kennedy took any discussion of hair. The president, simply put, was obsessed with his looks and especially with appearing physically fit, not least because he was secretly unhealthy and wanted to hide his many infirmities behind the carefully managed Kennedy/Bond/robust man-of-action mystique.

Hidden from the public was the fact that Kennedy wore a tightly bound corset to help support his poor back. (Also hidden from view were his crutches

President Kennedy in the limousine in Dallas, Texas, on Main Street, minutes before his assassination. Also in the limousine are Jackie Kennedy, Texas governor John Connally, and his wife, Nellie. Photograph by Walt Cisco of the *Dallas Morning News*, November 22, 1963.

and cane.) Tragically, the firm back brace likely aided in his assassination by preventing him from slumping over in the backseat of the presidential limousine after the assassin's initial shot to his back and neck, keeping the president upright for the kill shot to the head that followed.

Additionally, the method by which the president sought short-term relief from pain—through incessant drug use—was dangerous and disturbing, especially for the leader of the Free World. As Robert Dallek notes, the president was taking "steroids for his Addison's disease; painkillers for his back; antispasmodics for his colitis; antibiotics for urinary-tract infections; antihistamines for allergies; and, on at least one occasion, an antipsychotic for a severe mood change that Jackie Kennedy believed had been brought on by the

President John F. Kennedy and First Lady Jacqueline Kennedy arrive at the Inaugural Ball, by photographer Abby Rowe, January 20, 1961.

antihistamines." And all this in addition to the speed-laced "cocktails" from "Dr. Feelgood," aka "Miracle Max" Jacobson, who was on the Kennedy payroll, who followed the president on his travels in a separate plane, and whose needle of goodies was also enjoyed by Jackie and many celebrities of the day. In fact, the president took so many drugs—Jacobson made more than thirty "house calls" to the White House during Kennedy's presidency—that his brother Robert joked, "If a mosquito bites my brother, the mosquito dies."[165]

But there were three other significant elements to Kennedy's keen concern for public appearances. One was weight gain—Kennedy was paranoid about ever gaining a pound, and to track and control his weight he insisted on always traveling with a bathroom scale. Second, wanting always to look fresh and faultless, Kennedy changed outfits as often as four times a day—a new starched shirt, a different tie, another crisply pressed Brooks Brothers suit—meaning his longtime valet, George E. Thomas, was on constant call.[166] (Privately, Kennedy could be exceptionally untidy and unkempt, especially during the years before he held public office.) And third, his obsession with personal styling carried over to his carefully manicured chestnut-brown hair. His classic Ivy League hairstyle, with its meticulous side part and clean and casual sense of refinement, remains indelibly etched in the public memory of the man, as does the brunette bouffant of Jackie Kennedy, whose understated elegance made her a fashion icon. A quick internet search, some sixty years after the president's death, reveals scores of discussions devoted exclusively to Kennedy's hairstyle. "John F. Kennedy's

A quick internet search, some sixty years after the president's death, reveals scores of websites devoted exclusively to Kennedy's hairstyle.

Hairstyle: Get the Best Iconic Looks"; "The Beautiful Hair of JFK"; "15 Times John F. Kennedy's Hair Looked Impeccable"—such is the fascination with the Kennedy coif even today.

HAIR AND THE FAMED TV DEBATE

Hair and "impeccable looks," in fact, were factors in how JFK won the 1960 election in the first place, playing important roles in the signature event of the election campaign and one of the seminal moments in American political history—the first nationally televised debate between presidential candidates. The face-off occurred in Chicago on September 26, before a national audience of some 70 million viewers.[167]

Kennedy, the dapper junior senator from Massachusetts, looked cool and confident ("telegenic" would become the chic term), while Nixon, the vice

Photograph of the first presidential debate in 1960, with John F. Kennedy (left) and Richard Nixon (right). This was held in Chicago at CBS's WBBM-TV on September 26, 1960. Photograph by the Associated Press.

president, appeared sweaty and sick. Whereas Kennedy gazed straight into the camera and addressed the public with a sense of purpose, demonstrating both an early command of, as well as the power of, this blossoming medium, Nixon avoided the lens, seemed uneasy with the camera, and looked shifty and unsettled. The magnetic young senator, it turns out, had spent the days prior to the debate holed up in a hotel, relaxing and fielding question after question in preparation for the big night. Nixon, by contrast, had recently been hospitalized with an injured knee, was suffering from the flu, was running a fever, had visibly lost weight, was exhausted from "campaign cramming" to make up for lost time, and had even reinjured his bad leg upon arriving for the debate when he accidently banged it on the door of his limo.

Proving that bad situations can always get worse, Nixon then compounded the negative optics of the evening by wearing both a light-colored suit—which merely camouflaged him amid the light background of the stage and accentuated his already-ashen appearance—and a pancake-size layer of Lazy Shave. The latter was a drugstore makeup intended to hide one of his most unflattering features, but instead it caused him to perspire profusely before the intense studio lights. (Reportedly, when Nixon heard that Kennedy had refused the services of the TV studio's top makeup artist, who was amply equipped with professional stage makeup, the vice president did as well, opting instead for a quick coating of the cheap, over-the-counter substitute.) So noticeable was the vice president's sweating that the *Chicago Daily News* later wondered, "Was Nixon Sabotaged by TV Makeup Artists?"[168]

The feature unflattering to the vice president that necessitated the makeup was his late-afternoon growth of facial hair—his notorious five-o'clock shadow, which now appeared closer to six, given his already-pallid complexion. A beard may have been an asset to another president—Abraham Lincoln—but budding whiskers and the sweaty series of events they inspired proved to be Nixon's Waterloo that night. For compared to the tan, immaculately groomed,

For compared to the tan, immaculately groomed, and clean-shaven Kennedy, the drippy and dark-jowled vice president exuded a "menacing mug."

Marilyn's "Flirty Swoop"

A cheeky hair collector might pair some Kennedy locks with those snipped from the head of his reported paramour Marilyn Monroe just hours before she sang her seductive, breathy version of "Happy Birthday to You" to the president at Madison Square Garden in New York on May 19, 1962. Before fifteen thousand ecstatic attendees at the Democratic fundraiser dinner that evening, it was one of Monroe's last public appearances, for she would die less than three months later.

Robert Champion, famed hairdresser to the stars, had reportedly cut and styled Monroe's hair that day (some dispute this) at his salon on Fifth Avenue and even accompanied her to the event that evening, touching up her makeup and hair before she performed. He held Monroe's hand and helped the trembling actress inch her way up the stairs to the stage, which were nearly impossible for her to navigate in the skintight, flesh-colored, rhinestone-studded evening gown, which assistants had literally sewn her into backstage; the famed dress sold to Ripley's Believe It or Not! in 2016 for $4.8 million, breaking the record for the most expensive dress ever sold at auction.

Recently, a large, curled lock of her blonde hair kept by Champion, a sample described as a "flirty swoop," was offered for sale by Paul Fraser Collectibles. Accompanying the swoop was "a kiss" from Marilyn on an instant Polaroid photo of her, taken at the post-event party; as described in the sales lot, the image "captures Monroe smiling radiantly, perhaps in relief after getting through the performance, and bears her lipstick print in place of a signature on the reverse." The price in 2024 for the combined blonde locks and red lip-print photo? $315,000.

and clean-shaven Kennedy, the drippy and dark-jowled vice president exuded a "menacing mug."[169] To some radio listeners who merely heard the event (including Kennedy's running mate, Lyndon Johnson), Nixon had outdueled the junior senator and won the debate. Millions of TV viewers, however, saw it differently—*how* differently they saw it, and whether this radio-TV dichotomy is more myth than reality, has long been debated. The candidates' different styles and appearance obviously played a role in how the public perceived the debate and ultimately voted in the tightly contested general election, but whether "body politic" of this sort played just *a* role, instead of *the critical* role, continues to be questioned.[170]

The nationally broadcast event underscored nonetheless one formative, new fact about American life: the growing power of eyes over ears in the techno age of television. "The mushrooming TV audience saw [Nixon] as a truthless used-car salesman," concluded writer Hunter S. Thompson, "and they voted accordingly." Or as Nixon's running mate, Henry Cabot Lodge Jr., declared after the debate, "That son of a bitch just cost us the election."[171]

Hair, Image, and Infidelities

Considering Kennedy's keen attention to his public image, and to his personal appearance in particular, it's perhaps not surprising that he exhibited an uncontrollable habit of patting his head and smoothing his locks, retrieving and repositioning any tendril of hair that might dare to go rogue. For example, while the cameras were rolling but before the official start of his famed outdoor interview with CBS newsman Walter Cronkite in September 1963, the president was caught on film repeatedly smoothing his hair upset by the wind.

He did this as well just minutes before he was shot in Dallas in his open-topped limousine, when he was once again patting his head and smoothing his locks. Even at the critical time of the shooting, Kennedy instinctively reached for his head. "As is so often his habit," write Martin Dugard and Bill O'Reilly, "when something messes up his hair, John F. Kennedy's hand reflexively tries to pat the top of his head. But now the top of his head is gone."[172]

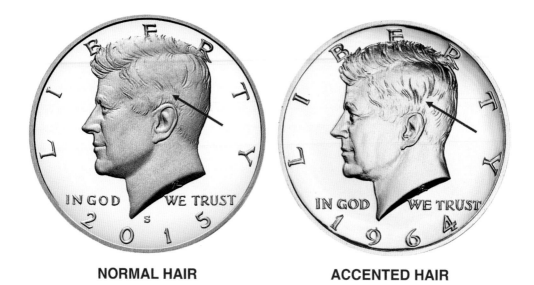

NORMAL HAIR   **ACCENTED HAIR**

Jackie contributed to this effort to maintain her husband's perfect coif, even after his death. In 1964, when the US Mint decided to release a special Kennedy half-dollar to memorialize the president, Jackie was instrumental in its final design, showcasing her husband's profile. Jackie was unhappy, though, with the first strike of some 100,000 coins. She thought the hair above the president's ear was too heavily accented, and so the design was tweaked and the remaining mintage released with less pronounced waves beneath the president's famed side part. Naturally, given its limited run, the first version of the coin, which subsequently became known as the "Accented Hair" Kennedy half-dollar, skyrocketed in value. Especially fine specimens of the coin have sold at auction for nearly $20,000.

The president's obsessive care for his hair would even factor into his extramarital affairs, which were as numerous as they were dangerous. "Kennedy's predatory personal behavior," writes historian Larry J. Sabato, "was as unrestrained and irresponsible as any ever engaged in by an occupant of the White

Two versions of the John F. Kennedy half-dollar, minted in memory of the slain president. After Jackie Kennedy expressed displeasure with the fuller depiction of the president's hair in the first strike of the coin, a new version was released with less hair beneath the president's famed side part. The first version of the coin then skyrocketed in value. Graphic by Oliver Pappas.

House," meaning "the potential for extortion by Kennedy's domestic and foreign enemies was huge, as was the risk of exposure."[173] Of special concern were the president's reckless trysts with women tied to Communist agents and Mafia bosses. But Jackie's health was equally at risk. As Sarah Bradford notes in her biography of the First Lady, "The underlying cause of [Jackie's miscarriage] and her subsequent history of childbearing—a stillbirth and two premature births—was almost certainly chlamydia, contracted from Jack as a result of his gonorrhea."[174]

Sex, in fact, was a central fact of Kennedy's existence, as critical to him as breathing and eating. "If I don't have sex every day, I get a headache," claimed

Singular photo of Robert (left) and John Kennedy (right) with Marilyn Monroe, at the party that followed the event where Monroe sang "Happy Birthday" to the president. This is widely cited as the only surviving photo of the president and Monroe together, since the FBI and Secret Service had attempted to confiscate all such images. Photograph by White House photographer Cecil W. Stoughton, May 19, 1962.

Kennedy, and so nothing was allowed to interfere with the president's "daily medicine." Not anything, noted essayist Caitlin Flanagan,

> . . . not his political ambitions, not issues of national security, not his Catholicism, not loyalty to his friends and his male relatives, not physical limitation or pain, not the risk of infecting any of his partners with the venereal disease that regularly plagued him, not fear of impregnating someone, not the potential for personal embarrassment, and certainly, certainly, not his marriage.[175]

Nineteen-year-old Mimi Alford was oblivious to all such concerns when she accepted an internship at the White House press office in the summer of 1962 and met Kennedy special assistant Dave Powers, a member of the president's "Irish Mafia" of key advisers.

One of Powers's responsibilities was the procuring of women for the president. Powers would shuttle them in and out of the White House, in and out of hotels, on and off the presidential support planes, and into this car or that car of the presidential motorcade—sometimes even hiding them on the floorboard of the cars. The reporters assigned to the president were willing participants in such subterfuge, exercising voluntary restraint and conveniently "looking the other way," as they did so poignantly during the presidency of Franklin Roosevelt, when they

President John F. Kennedy and President Manuel Prado Ugarteche of Peru, among others, walking through a doorway at the White House. Wearing glasses in the center is Dave Powers, the Special Assistant to the president who played a critical role in arranging Kennedy's many extramarital trysts. Photograph by Abbie Rowe, September 20, 1961.

refused to photograph or report on the president's crippled legs; it was all part of the unwritten pact that then existed between men of power and members of the press, a pact soon to vanish amid the contrails of Vietnam and Watergate.

On the fourth day of her internship, Mimi was approached by Powers and asked to join him and assorted girls from the White House for a midday dip in the presidential pool. She did, and there she met the president. She was then invited for after-hours drinks at the White House, where the president plied the teenager with daiquiris and offered to give her a private tour of the residence. "Blinded," in her words, "by the President's power and charisma," and now "tipsy" to boot, Mimi allowed him to seduce her—in Jackie's bedroom, no less, on the First Lady's bed. As usual for the president, the encounter was over quickly. Mimi had been a virgin. "I wouldn't describe what happened that night as making love," she later wrote.[176]

As Mimi and countless other women learned, extramarital sex to Kennedy was not love but lust.

As their affair progressed, Kennedy asked Mimi to do other things for him, such as sing silly school songs, share juicy gossip from the press office (the president was a notorious gossipmonger), and attend to something very dear to him: his hair. "The President was quite vain," she wrote years later in a book she released only reluctantly, after evidence of her affair finally leaked to the press:

"The President was quite vain."

> During the summer he would frequently summon me to the Oval Office and asked me to administer a hair treatment before one of his televised press conferences. The hair treatments were apparently a daily ritual that originated during the 1960 campaign. He insisted on using products only from Frances Fox, a company in upstate New York. He liked to lean back in his rocking chair and close his eyes while I massaged some tonic and an amber-colored ointment into his scalp. Then I would brush—never comb—it all into place. Sometimes a visitor would walk in while this was going on, and the President would signal for me to continue, and talk to his visitor as I worked away.[177]

Commissioned portrait of John F. Kennedy, painted by Aaron Shikler, 1970.

Having an affair with the president meant learning what Kennedy loved and what the president loathed. Treating his hair? This was most welcomed. Kissing—ever—on any occasion? This was verboten. Tellingly, during their eighteen-month affair, Mimi could not remember the president ever kissing her once, "not hello, not goodbye, not even during sex."[178] What she did remember was how indispensable Dave Powers was to their relationship and to the president in general; there was seemingly nothing Powers wouldn't do for his boss.

Even when Mimi was late with her period and relayed her concern to the president, who was unfazed by the news, Powers was at the ready to handle the situation. Within an hour of her discussion of the subject with the president, the phone rang for Mimi at her college dorm—it was Powers, with the name of a woman for Mimi to call to arrange for her visit to a doctor in New Jersey. Apparently, arranging for secret, illegal abortions was just another of the many services that Powers "facilitated" for the Catholic president. "There was no talk about what I wanted, or how I felt, or what the medical risks of an abortion might be," Mimi remembered.[179] Fortunately, she was not pregnant after all, simply late.

It was these experiences with the president's darker side—when Mimi wasn't doting on him with sex or hair treatments or gossip and silly school songs, when the president "felt a need to display his power over me"—that ranked among the worst times of their relationship, writes Mimi.[180] For example, at a party at Bing Crosby's house, the president pressured her to inhale amyl nitrite ("poppers"), a potentially dangerous stimulant that enhances sex for some users. She said she didn't want to, but Kennedy forced it under her nose nonetheless. Mimi's heart began racing, and her hands began trembling, leaving her terrified and running through the house in tears. Luckily, there was someone there to comfort her, to sit with her, until the effect of the drug wore off—no, not the president who had given her the drug, but Dave Powers.

Although humiliated on many occasions, Mimi continued her affair with the president through 1963. Kennedy had wanted her to join him on his fateful visit

Although humiliated on many occasions, Mimi continued her affair with the president through 1963.

to Dallas on November 22, but once Jackie decided to go as well, Mimi was nixed from the trip. The president then promised to phone her upon his return. Mimi reminded the president that she was now engaged to a fellow back home. "Remember, Mr. President, I'm getting married," she said. "I know that," Kennedy replied with a shrug. "But I'll call you anyway."[181]

Clearly, neither an engagement ring nor a marriage certificate held much sway with the president; to be fair, neither did a wedding ring nor an engagement matter much to Mimi either. But with Mimi's wedding on the horizon, and Jack's relationship with Jackie growing closer since the death of their prematurely born son, Patrick, on August 9, her affair with the president was plainly winding down. Kennedy sensed this as well, and so as an engagement gift and memento of their time together, Kennedy gave Mimi two gold-and-diamond pins—and a signed picture of himself. Their last meeting was at the Carlyle Hotel in New York on November 15.

The photo the president gave her was an iconic shot, showing him at the helm of his famed sailboat, relaxed and smiling confidently into the sun as he navigates through shimmering waters, with his famed chestnut-brown hair—which Mimi had lovingly cared for on so many occasions—blowing beautifully, perfectly, in the wind. It was the same precious head that the First Lady lovingly cradled in the back of the presidential limousine seven days later, as her husband lay dying from multiple gunshots, and then cut precious locks from in memory of her slain husband as he lay in his coffin. Ironically, for both the president's young widow and the president's young mistress, hair served as a final keepsake and remembrance of the man both women loved.

Hair served as a final keepsake and remembrance of the man both women loved.

It was a fitting denouement, the Kennedy saga in a nutshell—complicated and ugly and moving all in one.

President Kennedy sails aboard the U. S. Coast Guard yacht *Manitou* off the coast of Maine. Photograph by White House photographer Robert Knudsen, August 11, 1962.

1853
Benny

Robin
1953

CHAPTER FIVE

PARALLEL TRAGEDIES

THE PIERCES, THE BUSHES, AND THE

Death of a Child

---

*T*he political wonder boy was on the verge of becoming the youngest president in US history. He had charm and charisma, the vigor of youth, and, in the eyes of many then and some even now, he was the best-looking chief executive—with the best-looking hair—ever. No, not John F. Kennedy. Franklin Pierce (14th US president, 1853–57).

"Franklin Pierce was arguably the most handsome man ever to serve as president of the United States," writes historian and biographer Michael F.

Holt. "He was certainly one of the most amiable and congenial men to hold that office. Because of his popularity, personal charm, and family lineage, he enjoyed a meteoric political career in New Hampshire."[182] Born in Hillsborough, New Hampshire, in 1804, Pierce hailed from hardy, successful stock who were raised amid a spirit of service, sacrifice, and patriotism.

His father, Benjamin Pierce, was a Revolutionary War hero who had fought at the Battle of Bunker Hill, marched into Boston with George Washington's army upon the British evacuation of the city, served under Benedict Arnold at the battles of Ticonderoga and Bemis Heights, wintered with Washington at the hellish camp at Valley Forge, and served at West Point and along the Hudson River for the remainder of the war. He was even awarded a medal for distinguished service by Washington himself. Henceforth called "the General," Benjamin flourished amid the hill country of southwest New Hampshire, garnering great wealth and prominence. He was a successful farmer, a gregarious tavern owner (at a time when pubs were vital community and political hubs), a postmaster and sheriff, a member of the state legislature, and finally the governor of New Hampshire in 1827 and again in 1829.

Benjamin's charming son Franklin followed in his father's impressive footsteps. Born with striking dark eyes, a classical nose, luscious hair, and exactly the right number of digits on each hand and foot (he had escaped the bizarre affliction congenitally marking several members of the Pierce clan—six fingers on a hand and six toes on a foot—known as *polydactyly*), Franklin would succeed at nearly everything he attempted and become the youngest to accomplish nearly everything he accomplished.

"*Most important, he exuded a personal charm, an amiable temperament, and an instinctive human empathy.*"

He was elected to his state legislature at the mere age of twenty-four, named the state's Speaker of the House of Representatives at twenty-seven, elected to the US House of Representatives at twenty-eight, and became a member of the US Senate at thirty-two, making him the youngest US senator in American history at that time. He had also earned his law license along the way, becoming one of the mightiest trial lawyers in New Hampshire history, drawing throngs to the courtroom to hear his stirring arguments. He had a prodigious memory for faces and names, and "a deep, rich voice," notes Holt, "a trait that helped his political career because his audience could actually hear his unamplified voice at political rallies. Most important, he exuded a personal charm, an amiable temperament, and an instinctive human empathy."[183]

Young Pierce was even offered the post of US Attorney General, but he passed on the opportunity, and the chance to become the governor of New Hampshire as well, and went to war instead, serving as a brigadier general in the Mexican-American War (1846–48). True, his war experience was more Chaplin-like than Pattonesque. During his brigade's first battle, his horse was spooked, likely by an artillery burst, slamming the groin of the future president so violently against the saddle that Pierce briefly lost consciousness and began to fall from his mount, whereupon his horse tripped and fell atop him, severely injuring Franklin's knee, leaving him prostrate on the ground. During his second engagement, while marching his men through rough, murky terrain, Pierce twisted the injured knee, causing pain so severe that he once again passed out. Nor was his third campaign any more inspiring,

Portrait of President Franklin Pierce, by photographer Mathew Brady, circa 1855.

when he battled not the enemy but . . . an aggressive case of diarrhea, which kept him sidelined in a sick tent. But despite the mishaps and the ribbing he took ("Fainting Frank," he was dubbed by some; "The Hero of Many a Well-Fought Bottle," said others, in reference to Pierce's love of drink), his mettle was tested, and his successful maneuvering of two thousand five hundred men to the battlefront around Mexico City—with scores of wagons and heavy artillery, through one hundred fifty miles of enemy territory rife with snipers (his hat was shot off on one occasion)—was an impressive feat nonetheless, and for this he was rightly praised and honored.[184]

With a background like this, and with a winning personality and good looks to boot, it would have been shocking had Pierce *not* been tapped for a run for the most powerful office in the land, the presidency. And tapped he was by the Democratic Party for the election of 1852. He won twenty-seven of the thirty-one states, becoming the fourteenth president of the United States. At age forty-seven, Pierce was the youngest president yet elected in American history.

> *Just weeks away from taking the oath of office, thereby reaching the pinnacle of his political career, tragedy struck.*

But then, just weeks away from taking the oath of office, thereby reaching the pinnacle of his political career, tragedy struck. As Charles Dickens might have put it, "it was the best of times, it was the worst of times" for Franklin Pierce.

THE PIERCES' GREAT TRAGEDY

Heartache had haunted Pierce and his family before, but never like this. His first son, Franklin Pierce Jr., had died in 1836 after a mere three days of life—before Franklin, who was away in Washington, could even see him. Franklin's wife, Jane Means Appleton, was devastated by the loss, especially since she had already lost so many loved ones. Her brother John had died at age three when she was eleven; her father had died when she was thirteen; her brother William had died at twenty-two when she was twenty-four; and now her firstborn had died as well.

Fortunately, Franklin and Jane were blessed with another son three years later, and once again, Franklin was away in Washington when this son, Frank Robert, was born. Tragically, this son, too, would not live long—only four years. All of Jane's love and attention were then showered on their one remaining son, Benjamin ("Benny"), whom she doted on and watched over like a hawk, especially during Franklin's many absences from home, as when he served in the Mexican-American War. But tragedy tracked the family nonetheless, striking this time during the lame-duck period between Franklin's election to the presidency on November 2, 1852, and his inauguration on March 4, 1853.

Franklin, Jane, and Benny had been in Boston attending the funeral of Jane's uncle, who had died on New Year's Eve. Two days after the funeral, on January 6, the family boarded a train in nearby Andover for the short trip to their home in Concord, New Hampshire. It was a frigid, icy day, and the train's sole passenger car was blanketed white with frost. About a mile outside Andover, the car suddenly lurched amid a noisy, grinding sound—the car's front axle had broken off, derailing the car and disengaging it from the baggage carrier situated behind the engine; the passenger car spun around and then plunged some twenty feet down a rocky, steep embankment, finally landing upside down, broken "in pieces like a cigar box," reported a witness. Upon feeling the initial jolt of the derailment, Franklin had instinctively grabbed Jane, who was sitting next to him on a bench. He then immediately reached back to grab eleven-year-old Benny, who was traveling in the seat behind them. But his son slipped from his grasp.[185]

Jane and Franklin were battered in the accident but survived the ordeal. And their beloved

Daguerreotype of First Lady Jane Pierce with her son, Benjamin, taken several years before her husband's inauguration as president and Benjamin's death in 1853.

Benny, spotted nearby amid the wreckage, appeared fine as well—bloody and bruised, but otherwise okay. Like Lincoln in the immediate aftermath of the shooting at Ford's Theatre, when the president appeared uninjured and simply asleep in his chair in the presidential box, Benny just looked stunned or perhaps unconscious. The president-elect could see his son's beautiful face and delicate features. But like Lincoln again, whose hair was masking a mortal wound, Benny's front visage, locks and all, was hiding a horrible truth. For upon reaching Benny, as historian Peter A. Wallner notes,

> Pierce saw that the back of his son's head had been torn off by flying debris. Benny had been killed instantly. Pierce removed his cloak and covered the boy's body, but not before Jane had caught a glimpse of the grisly sight.[186]

"The poor boy's head was smashed to jelly," reported the *New York Times*.[187] In fact, with part of Benny's head missing, his brain was exposed for all to see, including his mother. Like First Lady Jackie Kennedy, First Lady Jane Pierce would now have to live, for the rest of her life, with that ghastly image of her loved one's mortally wounded skull.

Jane had always been tremulous and frail. Plagued by respiratory infections, coughs, fatigue, and an eating disorder that would likely be diagnosed as anorexia today, she was like "the heroine of a Victorian novel," states her official White House biography. "The gentle dignity of her face reflected her sensitive, retiring personality and physical weakness."[188] But this latest tragedy—the loss of her sole remaining son, in whom she and Franklin had placed so many hopes and dreams, and the horrible witnessing of his grisly death, no less—was too much for her.

Like the depression that overtook Mary Todd Lincoln and stole her sanity in the wake of her husband's assassination, Jane became lost in a fog of incessant grief that would never really lift, prematurely aging the forty-six-year-old First

Lady. "Jane was at times frantic in her grief which found vent in screams and piteous moans," records one account.[189] She sat in a stupor, overwhelmed by despair, and sought refuge in seclusion; she wore only black for two years, communicated on mourning stationery for three years, and at one point even took to writing letters to her dead son, apologizing for her supposed failings as a mother. (Mary Todd Lincoln had also sought to communicate with the dead, but she opted for a supposedly more direct route for communicating with her deceased children: medium-run séances in the White House.)

Most significantly, Jane's hatred for Washington and politics—which she had always despised—only grew in intensity. When she heard the news that her husband had been nominated for the presidency back in 1852, Jane had promptly fainted; she then openly prayed for her husband's defeat in the election. Benny's death, in her mind, was simply part of the nightmare she long feared was coming because of Franklin's ascent up the ladder of national politics. From her perspective, set firmly in the Calvinist tradition of predestination by which everything happened according to divine will, God had taken her beloved Benny for a particular reason: so her husband could serve the country unfettered, unburdened by a family and the responsibilities of a father. Put plainly, the death of her final son, as Jane saw it, was just another

Portrait of Franklin Pierce, by George Peter Alexander Healy, 1853.

sacrifice on the altar of Franklin's political career. Franklin, to some degree, likely believed this as well, which perhaps is why instead of *swearing* the oath to uphold the office of the presidency with his hand on a Bible on Inauguration Day, he merely *affirmed* his loyalty to the US Constitution with his hand on a law book. He dared not provoke the Almighty any further.

So distraught was Jane that she was unable to attend the reception for her husband held after the inauguration. Nor was she able to part with the one thing she had intended to give Franklin to carry with him during the swearing-in ceremony: a snippet of Benny's hair, which she had preserved as a keepsake—she just couldn't part with this precious, tangible remnant of her beloved lost, last son.[190] In fact, she never was able to accept the duties and responsibilities traditionally assumed by First Ladies, and so a girlhood friend and eventual relative by marriage stood in for her and played the role of Washington hostess during her husband's term as president.

Franklin, too, was devastated by Benny's death, but he now felt the added burden of guilt for his wife's worsening emotional state. "It was enough to break one's heart when Mr. Pierce would come into her room nearly bent double by his bruises & muscular strains [from the train accident] and throw himself on the bed and mingle his woe with hers," noted Jane's cousin. "There is but one opinion about him: that he is one of the noblest and most tender hearted of human beings."[191]

"There is but one opinion about him: that he is one of the noblest and most tender hearted of human beings."

Clouding the start of Pierce's presidency even further was the fact that Jane was not the only key person missing from the presidential entourage. Gone as well was his vice president, William Rufus DeVane King, the longtime housemate and rumored paramour of future president and lifelong bachelor James Buchanan, who would succeed Pierce as the fifteenth president of the United States. ("Miss Nancy and Aunt Fancy" was what a sardonic Andrew Jackson dubbed the fastidious vice president and refined future president, whom some have called—despite the lack of hard evidence—America's "first gay president." One congressman referred to them as "Buchanan & his wife"; others referred to them as "Siamese Twins" and called the vice president Buchanan's "better half.")[192]

King was in Cuba, avidly seeking a cure for the tuberculosis that was killing him, and only by a special act of Congress was he able to take the oath of office from his sickbed in a foreign land (the only vice president to do so). It hardly mattered—King died a few weeks later, a day after returning to his plantation near Selma, Alabama, a city he had cofounded. This left Pierce without a vice president for his entire term of office, further

blackening the cloud already shadowing Pierce at the start of his presidency.

So, as the country welcomed its new leader, it did so with a heavy heart. And as the country struggled to prosper, to expand westward to new territories, and to straddle the ever-widening fissures over the issue of slavery, Pierce battled in tandem in his personal life to keep his emotions intact, his marriage together, and his lifelong love of liquor in check. He struggled on all fronts, and his administration, in the end, would be deemed a failure, mainly due to his support for the Kansas-Nebraska Act of 1854. This act allowed settlers to decide for themselves whether to permit slavery and led to open warfare in "Bleeding Kansas" between pro- and antislavery factions, which merely fanned the flames of national discord and angered both sides of the political aisle. Outraged were Northerners who wanted to curb if not outright abolish slavery, and equally incensed were Pierce's fellow Democrats, because the president's policies paved the way for the rise of the Republican Party and Abraham Lincoln, whose election to the presidency in 1860 finally sparked the conflagration all had feared: the Civil War. The Kansas-Nebraska Act became an indelible stain on Pierce's administration.

Franklin Pierce in uniform, photograph by Mathew Brady, 1852.

Pierce's presidency was—in a word—disastrous. The charming and dashing wonder boy with the courtly manners, whose youth and vigor had wooed a nation just four years earlier, when he amazingly delivered his inaugural address by memory, was now, in 1857, rejected by his own party for a possible second term in office. "Anybody but Pierce" had become the reigning sentiment of the day, with many branding him the worst president in American history. It was an astounding about-face in political and personal fortunes.

"Get drunk," he said, and get drunk he did, freely and frequently, giving way to the demon that had haunted him for so long.

When asked what he would do in his postpresidential days, Pierce replied with a candor unimaginable for a politician today. "Get drunk," he said, and get drunk he did, freely and frequently, giving way to the demon that had haunted him for so long. Pierce did, during the last twelve years of his life after leaving the presidency in 1857, have some productive periods: he and Jane traveled to Europe, hoping it would improve her health—she finally died from tuberculosis in 1863; during the Civil War, he argued publicly for a defense of Washington and the North from any invasion by the South, but castigated Lincoln for his suspension of civil liberties and any Northern notions of a vengeful subjugation of a defeated South; he renewed his deep friendship with writer Nathaniel Hawthorne, whom he had befriended during their days at Bowdoin College and then cared for and was traveling with when the writer died in 1864; and he bought and farmed eighty acres of land along the New Hampshire shoreline.

Through it all, however, one constant remained: his always avid and active affection for booze. With few barriers now to brace him from the alcoholic tide, the wave of his addiction soon overwhelmed him, leading to the cirrhosis of the liver that finally killed Pierce on October 8, 1869.

Pierce might have died, but debate over his hair lived on. In fact, the White House–related locks spawning the most scrutiny and scuttlebutt over the longest time belong not to Donald Trump but to Franklin Pierce.

"Handsome Frank" was Pierce's moniker, and for good reason. He was an immaculate dresser, exhibited courtly manners, and enjoyed magnificent hair that he frequently didn't comb; like a Hollywood star, he often wore it tousled or cascading down his forehead. His hairstyle, in fact, was one of the most commented-on characteristics of the man, living *or* dead.

In 1868, a year before Pierce died, a young piano player met the former president in a hotel lounge and noted Pierce's "personable face" and—of course—his hair.

He was "a tall, stout man with a flat face and rather long hair which hangs down over his forehead," the young man remembered. The former president's locks were even the focus of attention upon his death in 1869, when mourners passing his open coffin frequently commented on "his mass of curly black hair, somewhat tinged by age, but which was still combed on a deep slant over his wide forehead."[193]

Even today, Pierce's lustrous locks are well delineated for the public in various ways. For example, his striking mane is on full display in the bronze statue of Pierce that was revealed in downtown Rapid City, South Dakota, in 2007, as part of the City of Presidents campaign that local leaders initiated in 2000 to build civic pride in their national heritage; the statue's location was unfortunate but all too fitting— outside a pub. The president's impressive hair is also the defining feature of the special coin depicting Pierce that the US Mint released in 2010 as part of its Presidential Dollar series; the president is portrayed in striking form— high cheekbones, harmonious eyes, straight nose, and, of course, deeply contoured, long,

A gold coin depicting Franklin Pierce that the US Mint released in 2010 as part of its Presidential Dollar series.

wavy locks. He is even depicted with a hip, popped-up collar. He was similarly well represented the following year, when Madame Tussauds, the famed wax museum (now closed) in Washington, DC, debuted its US Presidents Gallery. A reporter for the *Dallas Morning News* who attended the 2011 opening was dumbstruck by the wax portrayal of the "worst president in US history." Who knew, he quipped, that Franklin Pierce "was a total stud"?[194]

Presidential scholars, however, who are forever on the lookout for clues, *any* clues, into their subject's character and personality, have long puzzled over Pierce's striking mane. Was the president's tousled hairstyle just a quirk of vanity, they've wondered, or was it a deliberate fashion statement by the president of the United States? Or was it a sign of neglect in a man otherwise careful about his suave and dapper appearance?

> *Presidential scholars, however, who are forever on the lookout for clues, any clues, into their subject's character and personality, have long puzzled over Pierce's striking mane.*

The great hair debate "came to a head" in 2008, when the New Hampshire Historical Society won at auction a letter written by Pierce's wife in 1857 that references Franklin's luscious locks. "Today," writes Jane, "Mr. Pierce has met the citizens of Norfolk and after the fatigue is quietly lying on the sofa by a bright fire with Miriam [Jane's maid] brushing his hair soporifically." Although the evidence is far from conclusive, the letter, says the historical society, "leads one to suspect that the vanity Pierce showed for his appearance extended to his hair as well."[195]

THE BUSHES' GREAT TRAGEDY

Exactly one hundred years after the death of Benny Pierce in 1853, another future First Lady and future president of the United States struggled to cope

---

Franklin Pierce, oil on canvas, painted by artist George Peter Alexander Healy, 1853.

with the tragic death of a child. It was the spring of 1953, and George H. W. Bush (41st US president, 1989–93) and his wife, Barbara, were among the many ambitious young couples who had moved to the scrub town of Midland, Texas.

Here up-and-coming businessmen and entrepreneurs like George, with their dutiful wives like Barbara, lived in cookie-cutter homes, all perfect in their sameness, in a quaint community called Easter Egg Row (so named for the vibrant color each house was painted). The couple's goal was simple and widely shared: to become as rich as possible off that black gold called oil, and many, like the Bushes, accomplished just that.

The men worked hard, and their wives did, too, as homemakers and moms. "If your husband wanted you to do something, you'd do it, and gladly. I still think there's nothing wrong with this," said Barbara years later, exhibiting

that plain-talking and traditionalist mindset that would later distinguish her as First Lady.[196] But daily life was especially hard on the women, for the men were mostly gone, traveling or prospecting or problem-solving in the oil fields, leaving the women to deal with every mishap and challenge on the home front. For example, on one occasion, when their son, George W., got in trouble at school and the principal spanked the future US president, Barbara was furious. She stormed

The portrait of Pauline Robinson "Robin" Bush that hung in the Bushes' Texas homes, painted by Louise Altson, 1953. As the artist recalled in 1987, "That's the one portrait I painted with tears." Photo courtesy of the George H. W. Bush Presidential Library and Museum.

down to the principal's office and announced, "My husband's going to kill you. He's out of town, but he's coming home to kill you immediately."[197]

But in the spring of 1953, one issue arose that George, then twenty-eight years old, could not entirely leave to his wife. Barbara noticed bruises on the body of their three-year-old daughter, "Robin" (Pauline Robinson), bruises that should have gone away with time. But they didn't. A doctor ran tests and promptly announced the shocking results: Robin had an advanced case of leukemia (cancer of the blood) and perhaps only weeks to live. George and Barbara were floored. Neither of them had even heard of the disease, which was still relatively unknown. Plus, it was a time when cancer was only whispered about, seldom openly discussed. Now it was killing their precious daughter—and rapidly.

Open to any treatment with even the slightest chance for success, Barbara and George flew Robin to the Sloan Kettering Institute for Cancer Research in New York, where early forms of chemotherapy were underway. (They did so on the advice of George's uncle, Dr. John Walker, who was then president of Memorial Hospital, adjacent to the institute.) A seemingly endless array of tests and probes followed, and through it all, little Robin smiled, and her perkiness rarely waned; she laughed and played games from her hospital bed and reportedly inspired everyone who came her way. But she suffered great pain in the following weeks and months, and her condition only worsened.

Barbara mandated one rule for anyone in her daughter's presence: no crying.

By the fall of 1953, Robin was clearly dying, and George couldn't take it. He had seen death up close during his service in World War II, but he couldn't

George and Barbara Bush with their children, George and Robin, at the rodeo grounds in Midland, Texas, October 1950.

stand to witness the dying of his daughter and so avoided situations when he'd see her in pain. This meant that, while he flew back and forth between New York and Texas to tend to his fledgling oil business, the difficult task of caring for Robin's daily needs once again fell to Barbara. And no matter how heartbreaking the moment, during those difficult times when Robin was panicked and screaming in pain, Barbara mandated one rule for anyone in her daughter's presence: no crying.

Tears from anyone other than Robin were banned from the hospital room. "I made up my mind that there would be no tears around Robin," wrote Barbara, "so I asked people who cried to step out of her room. I didn't want to scare our little girl." In fact, George excused himself so often, saying he had to use the bathroom, that Robin thought her daddy had a potty problem—it became a running joke in the family. But no, noted Barbara, George did not have the weakest bladder in the world. "He just had the most tender heart."[198]

So, day after day, week after week, month after month, Barbara lived by her daughter's side, combing her hair and calming her nerves as the increasingly frail child, now blackened with bruises and blanketed with open sores, endured still more procedures, treatments, and probes, including blood transfusions and painful bone marrow tests.

Barbara was the rock that stabilized the family during the half-year ordeal, never breaking down, never weakening, keeping her emotions in check. "It was beyond strength," wrote biographer Richard Ben Cramer of Barbara during those days. "It was heroic, an act of will and love."[199] And Barbara remained strong to the very end, when finally, on October 11, 1953, on the brink of her fourth birthday, Robin died. She died in Barbara's arms, as her mother stroked her beautiful blonde curls. "For one last time I combed her hair," noted Barbara, performing the same simple act of caring devotion that both Lincoln and Coolidge had done as they sat beside the bodies of their dead children, mourning their loss. Barbara had combed Robin's hair hundreds of times in her daughter's short life, but this time was different, even life-changing for the future First Lady. "I never felt the presence of God more strongly than at that moment," she later wrote.[200]

Robin's buoyant blonde curls had been a particular source of pride for the family quickly filling out with boys, which was something George H. W. referenced in a poignant letter to his mother a few years after Robin's death:

> There is about our house a need. The running, pulsating restlessness of the four
> boys as they struggle to learn and grow; their athletic chests and arms and legs . . .
> all this wonder needs a counterpart. We need some starched crisp frocks to go with
> all our torn-kneed blue jeans and helmets. We need some soft blond hair to offset
> those crew cuts. We need a doll house to stand firm against our forts and rackets and
> thousand baseball cards. . . . We need a girl.[201]

What he missed most of all, among the rough-and-tumble of his boys, was her "certain softness"—and, of course, her darling curls:

> She was patient—her hugs were just a little less wiggly. Like [the boys], she'd climb
> in to sleep with me, but somehow she'd fit. She didn't boot and flip and wake me

Chief Justice William Rehnquist administering the oath of office to President George H. W. Bush
during inaugural ceremonies at the US Capitol on January 20, 1989. Photographer unknown.

up with pug nose and mischievous eyes a challenging quarter-inch from my sleeping face. No—she'd stand beside our bed till I felt her there. Silently and comfortable, she'd put those precious, fragrant locks against my chest and fall asleep. Her peace made me feel strong, and so very important.

"My daddy" had a caress, a certain ownership which touched a slightly different spot than the "Hi, Dad" [from the boys] I love so much. But she is still with us. We need her and yet we have her. We can't touch her, and yet we can feel her.[202]

Fifty years later, Bush tried reading this letter aloud to biographer Jon Meacham, and he couldn't do it without breaking down. He began "crying so hard that he had difficulty catching his breath."[203]

In fact, for decades George refused to discuss the death of his daughter—with Barbara or with anyone—admitting years later, "I was too weak to, I guess. Barbara could." In the moments before she died, the blue-eyed Robin had looked up at her father and muttered a line that George would remember and forever repeat to family and loved ones thereafter: "I love you more than tongue can tell." George kept a photo of Robin on his desk for the rest of his life, and on the day that his son launched Operation Iraqi Freedom, beginning the invasion of Iraq in March 2003, and knowing the strain his son was now under as a wartime president, George sent his son a simple note: "Remember Robin's words, 'I love you more than tongue can tell.'"[204]

And though George was always loath to discuss publicly this painful chapter in his life, he could muster the courage to do so when necessary. For example, during the 1980 presidential campaign, when a journalist grilled him on whether he, given his wealth, had ever dealt with a "personal difficulty," little Robin shot immediately to mind. "Have you ever sat and watched your child die?" George asked. "I did, for six months." The journalist was stunned silent; the interview was over.[205]

Clearly, the loss of Robin was the most painful chapter in the Bushes' life, but it was a chapter with silver linings, according to Barbara. First, it brought Barbara and Georgie (George W.)—the oldest Bush child and the one most like his mother in her affable, quick-witted, frank-talking ways—very close, cementing a special mother-son bond, especially in the days right after Robin's death. As happened with Jane Pierce and her relationship with her remaining son, Benny, in the wake of her second son's death, Barbara needed an immediate outlet for her mothering impulse after the death of Robin, and Georgie became the chief focus of her attention. In fact, Barbara's attention grew so intense that "she kind of smothered me," he remembered.[206]

But Georgie would play an even larger role in the family dynamics at this critical time. He was both the family clown and the family cheerleader, and his humor, youthful innocence, and unhindered way of remembering his sister had a salutary effect on the family in a dire time of need. He helped everyone to heal and to come to terms with their loss. For example, while watching a football game shortly after Robin's death, Georgie announced that he wished he were his sister, at that very moment. The adults around him froze in terror at the mere mention of Robin. George finally broke the awkward silence and asked his son why he wanted to be his sister. Because "I bet she can see the game better from up there than we can here," he said. Everyone laughed. As Barbara would later write, Georgie "made it okay" for her and her family and their friends to mention Robin and talk about her openly once again, and "that helped us a great deal."[207]

The adults around him froze in terror at the mere mention of Robin.

Not that the death of his sister didn't affect George W. He suffered repeated nightmares after her funeral, and tears still welled in his eyes decades later, when asked about his sister during his campaign for the presidency in the election of 2000. "Forty-six years later, those minutes [surrounding the death of his sister] remain the starkest memory of my childhood," he would write, "a sharp pain in the midst of an otherwise happy blur."[208] The *Washington*

Post zeroed in on this chapter in his life during its extensive interview with the candidate:

> [S]ome close to the Bushes do see the death of his sister as a singular event in George W.'s childhood, helping to define him and how he would deal with the world. Life would be full of humor and driven by chance. And it would be something approached with a certain fatalism. Even as an adolescent, Bush would tell his friends, "You think your life is so good and everything is perfect; then something like this happens and nothing is the same," recalls John Kidde, a high school classmate.[209]

This perception and approach to life spurred Bush "to live his life in the present, 'in chapters' as his brother Marvin would say, seizing opportunities as they came without fretting about what tomorrow might bring."[210]

"She felt bad because she had straight, brunette hair instead of the blonde curls Robin had."

Robin's legacy had quite a different effect on George's sister, Dorothy (called "Doro"), who was born in 1959, six years after Robin's death. "It's a strange thing to mourn someone you never met," she later explained. Such grieving, in fact, can take many forms, and in Doro's case, she even felt pangs of inadequacy while living in the shadow of the beloved lost Robin. And what especially triggered her angst? Robin's beautiful blonde hair. "She felt bad because she had straight, brunette hair instead of the blonde curls Robin had," noted biographer Susan Page, blonde curls which everyone in the family had adored.[211]

The other silver lining, in Barbara's eyes, involved her marriage. Often the death of a child can doom a marriage and lead to divorce, and though the death of Robin certainly tested their relationship and Christian faith, the experience ultimately deepened their relationship and their spirituality, and brought them closer together. "Because of Robin," concluded Barbara, "George and I love every living human more."[212]

GRIEF AND ITS CONSEQUENCES

But despite the eventual silver linings and final acceptance of Robin's loss, the drawn-out ordeal had been extremely difficult on the family, and it was downright devastating to Barbara. Physically exhausted and emotionally spent from the many months of suppressing her emotions, Barbara finally—upon the death and burial of Robin—fell apart. Like fellow First Ladies Jane Pierce and Mary Todd Lincoln before her, despair overwhelmed her, and she fell into a serious depression. This mandated a change in the Bushes' marital roles: it was now George's time to take the lead, to manage the home front, and to be the strong one for the family.

Adding to Barbara's stress was a side effect of the trauma that no one could have predicted—Barbara's light-brown hair began to gray and evolve into her signature snowy white, giving her that grandmotherly appearance that the world came to know so well when she served as First Lady of the United States some forty years later, when her husband became president of the United States.

As happened with First Lady Jane Pierce in the wake of Benny's death, stress and depression would prematurely age the future First Lady. As biographer Susan Page notes, a November 20, 1988, story in the *Los Angeles Times* about the new First Lady appears to be the first widely published mention of this supposedly sensational follicle transformation. "Their daughter, Robin, died of leukemia at the age of 4," reported the paper. "Barbara, then 30, 'nearly fell apart,' she has said, and friends recall that her hair

Former First Lady Barbara Bush at the LBJ Presidential Library, photographed by Lauren Gerson, November 15, 2012.

turned white virtually overnight." Although details in the story were wrong—in fact, Barbara was twenty-eight, Robin only three—the story metastasized like the cancer that had robbed Robin of her life, with newspapers and magazines repeating the story ad infinitum. The *New York Times* ran with the story, errors and all, on January 15, 1989: "Friends recall that her hair turned white virtually overnight."[213]

"That's baloney," Barbara told Page, when the latter asked her about the changing color of her hair. According to Barbara's telling of the story, she was actually thirty-five when her hair began seriously turning gray, and the color was further affected by her endless hours of swimming laps in the pool. "It turned green in the chlorine," remembered Barbara, and "the combination of chlorine with hair coloring was sometimes catastrophic," wrote Page.[214] Her hair, at one point, even turned orange. Barbara then let nature take its course and allowed her snowy white hair to flourish unencumbered. (See Chapter Six for a more detailed discussion of this story.)

Her hair, at one point, even turned orange.

BODY-SHAMING A FIRST LADY

Given the constant scrutiny that the First Family receives, it's perhaps not surprising that Barbara Bush, the white-haired First Lady with the matronly looks and stout silhouette, became the topic of endless murmurings and the butt of endless jokes. *Didn't she look more like George's mother than his wife?* In fact, during George's run for the presidency, this whispered concern, "What to do about Bar?"—about her grandmotherly appearance—circulated among not just the campaign staff but the Bush family itself. As a sister-in-law remembered, there was even a family conclave, *without* Barbara present, when "they considered whether they should urge her to lose weight, to color her hair, to wear more fashionable clothes."[215] Barbara's body politic, like Lincoln's, had become a political issue, a possible liability, and a frequent topic of discussion and debate.

Obviously, the situation was a delicate one. George, after all, looked younger than his actual years; Barbara, on the other hand, looked not just her age but . . .

older, something the national media handled with little grace. Even women reporters of the time were brutally insensitive. "Mrs. Bush, people say your husband is a man of the eighties," sniggered Jane Pauley of *The TODAY Show*, "and you're a woman of the forties. What do you say to that?" Barbara was devastated by the question, but she rebounded brilliantly, mustering a masterful reply: "Oh, you mean people think I look forty? Neat."[216]

Barbara, in fact, became famous for her zingers and self-deprecating ways, which I had the good fortune to witness firsthand during a charming, chance dinner I had with her in the fall of 1980, when she made a quick stopover in Wisconsin while campaigning on behalf of

"*My mail tells me a lot of fat, white–haired, wrinkled ladies are tickled pink.*"

President George H. W. Bush with First Lady Barbara Bush, standing with Boris Yeltsin and his wife, Naina Yeltsina, at the North Portico driveway of the White House in Washington, DC. Photograph by Mark Reinstein, June 17, 1992.

the Reagan-Bush ticket. "My mail tells me a lot of fat, white-haired, wrinkled ladies are tickled pink," she remarked, repeating a line she had used on the stump several times but losing none of her genuineness in the process. "I think it makes them feel better about themselves."

Her good-naturedness and down-to-earth manner even stole the show on a highly controversial stage, ten years later, at the spring 1990 commencement ceremony at Wellesley College in Massachusetts, one of the most prestigious women's colleges in the country. Liberal students at the institution had protested Barbara's selection as commencement speaker. "We are outraged by this choice," read a protest petition. "To honor Barbara Bush as a commencement speaker is to honor a woman who has gained recognition through the achievements of her husband, which contradicts what we have been taught over the last four years at Wellesley." The protest gained traction and then went global, spawning an international debate and more than 7,000 articles in newspapers and magazines in countries the world over.

Barbara, however, refused to be "canceled" and went on with the speech, opening with a self-deprecating remark that pivoted on what had become, for good or ill, her most distinguishing feature: her hair. "Now I know your first choice for [speaker] today was Alice Walker . . . known for *The Color Purple*," she told the crowd of five thousand. "Instead, you got me—known for the color of my hair!" The crowd laughed, relaxing Barbara and the tense audience alike, setting the stage for her brilliant home run. "And who knows?" said the First Lady. "Somewhere out in this audience may even be someone who will one day follow in my footsteps and

President George W. Bush and his mother, former First Lady Barbara Bush, in the Oval Office, October 3, 2003.

preside over the White House as the president's spouse." And, she added, "*I wish him well!*" The audience exploded with laughter and applause—Barbara had triumphed against the odds.[217]

Nonetheless, the body-shaming Barbara experienced was ruthless and unrelenting, as she and her looks became frequent targets of late-night television. Comedian Phil Hartman repeatedly played her in drag on *Saturday Night Live*, and Barbara's grandmotherly appearance nearly always formed the punch line of the jokes. "Tell me," Barbara/Hartman was asked when George was running for the presidency in 1988, "are you proud of your son?" The interviewer in the skit then fawns over the comedienne playing the fetching Elizabeth Dole, a one-time leader of the departments of labor and transportation and the wife of US senator Robert Dole, who was running against Bush for the Republican nomination that year. "Heavens! Have they ever called you Wonder Woman?" gushes the interviewer. Turning then to the matronly Hartman, the interviewer quips, "Now, Barbara, I understand you've written a book about the family cocker spaniel and you're working on a rug." Comedian Robin Williams continued the assault after Bush won the election. "President Bush has only been president a few short months," he cracked in 1989, "and already he has managed to put his wife on the dollar bill."[218]

Comedian Phil Hartman repeatedly played her in drag on Saturday Night Live, and Barbara's grandmotherly appearance nearly always formed the punch line of the jokes.

In the end, however, it's not just the White House, a child's tragic death, and issues concerning hair that the Bushes and the Pierces have in common. For Barbara Bush was not only the wife of a US president and the mother of a US president—a distinction she shared with Abigail Adams—but she was also a relative of yet another US president. Her maiden name before becoming Mrs. George H. W. Bush? Barbara *Pierce*.

CHAPTER SIX

FOLLICLE FORENSICS

SOLVING PRESIDENTIAL MYSTERIES THROUGH

Science and DNA

Although First Lady Barbara Bush and President Franklin Pierce had genetic ties—they were fourth cousins, three times removed, according to the New Hampshire Historical Society—he was not the only historical figure to whom Barbara Bush was tied. The First Lady shared a commonality with numerous luminaries from the past, including Sir Thomas More; King Henry IV of France; Mary, Queen of Scots; Emperor Shah Jahan (builder of the Taj Mahal); Marie Antoinette; US senator John McCain; and even a teenage student from the first century who's discussed in the Talmud. The tie that binds them, however, is *hair*.

THE MARIE ANTOINETTE SYNDROME

Each of these historical figures reportedly experienced the same stress-related follicle transformation associated with Barbara Bush. Known in medical circles as *Canities subita*, Latin for the sudden graying/whitening of hair, the phenomenon is popularly called the "Marie Antoinette syndrome." For the French queen's hair had allegedly suffered this same transformation in 1793, dramatically changing from strawberry blonde to white right before her beheading, due to the stress of her imprisonment and pending execution. Sir Thomas More and Mary, Queen of Scots, reportedly experienced the same sudden whitening or graying before their beheadings in 1535 and 1587, respectively. King Henry IV of France supposedly did as well, after the horrific St. Bartholomew's Day Massacre of thousands of Protestants by Catholics that followed his wedding in August 1572. Emperor Shah Jahan reportedly did, too, after the death of his beloved wife in 1631, for whom he built the Taj Mahal. Bombing victims during World War II and prisoners of war in Vietnam (like McCain) reportedly suffered this same follicular fate.[219]

As discussed in the last chapter, Barbara Bush downplayed the swiftness and source of her premature aging and hair-color change that caused such consternation, mockery, and debate ("What to do about Bar?") during her husband's run for the presidency in 1988 and her subsequent tenure in the White House as First Lady (1989–93). She attributed the follicle transformation to swimming, chlorine, bad hair coloring, and the common aging process, to seemingly anything but that horrible, painful chapter in her life when her child died. But despite her protestations to the contrary, a dramatic transformation in her looks—to her

She attributed the follicle transformation to swimming, chlorine, bad hair coloring, and the common aging process.

hair, especially—was evident to family and friends alike. Even her son George W. Bush mentioned the dramatic change in his mother's appearance that occurred after the death of his sister, and he directly tied the start of her premature aging to the stress she had suffered from his sister's protracted illness. "After seven months of staying strong, Mother cratered," he remembered. "She suffered bouts of depression that would plague her periodically. At twenty-eight years old, her dark brown hair started to turn white."[220]

For centuries, doctors have debated and doubted the veracity of this so-called syndrome and the role that stress may play in such pathophysiological changes. Many scientists have outright dismissed the possibility of this sort of follicle morphing, relegating such claims to legend and folklore. "It is in fact medically impossible," proclaimed a *Live Science* article in 2012. "There is no mechanism by which hair could organically turn white, either suddenly or overnight."[221]

Others, like dermatologist David Orentreich, believe the metamorphosis is an optical illusion stemming from a very real condition, the one that caused Jada Pinkett Smith to lose her hair. When comedian Chris Rock joked about her baldness at the 2022 Academy Awards, her husband, Will Smith, dramatically mounted the stage and slapped the comic, generating not only a collective gasp from the live TV audience but an informative discussion of this incurable condition: alopecia. Many considered Rock's gibe not only in bad taste but surprising, given his documentary, *Good Hair* (2009), in which he had traced the Black community's complex history with hair and hair's tangled role in race relations. "If your hair is relaxed, white people are relaxed, but if your hair is nappy, they're not happy." Such pressures and perceptions (courtesy of comedian Paul Mooney) were discussed by Rock, along with actress Nia Long's even pithier quip: "The lighter, the brighter, the better!"[222]

Concerning alopecia and the so-called "Marie Antoinette syndrome," Dr. Orentreich writes,

> If someone has salt-and-pepper hair—a mixture of gray and black—and they develop
>
> alopecia areata, the dark hairs can fall out quickly. . . . So it appears that [the person

Sketch of Marie Antoinette with chopped hair as she's wheeled to her execution, drawn quickly by famed painter Jacques-Louis David, October 16, 1793.

has] gone gray overnight. . . . It's conceivable for a person who has a tendency for alo-pecia areata to go through a stressful experience which makes it flare up and the first thing that happens is their dark hair falls out. . . . And that can happen quickly—in days or weeks—leaving just the gray hair.

But the actual hair, he says, is not changing color, for "you can't lose pigment in your hair. Once [the hair] leaves your scalp, it's nonliving; it's dead."[223]

Orentreich concedes that this syndrome is "appealing on a literary or poetic level that a person's experience could be so severe or terrifying that they age overnight." In fact, adds Dr. Alexander Navarini, it "has captured storytellers' imagination like few other afflictions," occurring "to protagonists as a sign of grave sorrow in religious texts as early as the Talmud," when a teenage student supposedly worked so hard and worried so much that his hair suddenly turned white.[224]

Indeed, artists through the ages, from poets and dramatists to novelists and filmmakers, have been drawn to this affliction, using it as a conven-ient metaphor for extreme shock, fright, stress, or grief. Shakespeare, for example, has Falstaff note in *Henry IV, Part 1* (1598) that, when "Worcester is stolen away to-night: thy father's beard is turn'd white with the news," and some two centuries later, in his famed poem *Marmion* (1808), Sir Walter Scott warns:

> *Artists through the ages . . . have been drawn to this affliction, using it as a convenient metaphor for extreme shock, fright, stress, or grief.*

> Danger, long travel, want, or woe,
> Soon change the form that best we know—
> For deadly fear can time outgo,
> And blanch at once the hair.

In Edgar Allan Poe's short story "A Descent into the Maelstrom" (1841), a young but old-looking fisherman experiences a similar follicle transformation after battling the terrifying, sucking waters and whipping winds around the black, tunneling eye of an enormous whirlpool, and in Bram Stoker's classic, *Dracula* (1897), young Jonathan Harker's hair is whitened overnight from the horror of his wife's encounter with the vampire. Terror is often the spur of this metamorphosis of the mane, as depicted in the Steven Spielberg horror flick *Poltergeist* (1982). After entering the spirit world through a portal in her home to rescue her daughter, who had been kidnapped by poltergeists, the mother returns safely, but not without a stigmata-like mark of her harrowing experience: the mother's dark hair is now streaked grayish white.

But could this affliction, so artfully and prolifically rendered through the ages, actually be real and not just an optical illusion? Dr. Navarini, writing in 2009, at least left the door open to an actual medical explanation. "The mystery still shrouding this rare syndrome has yet to be explained."

Until now?

In 2020 Harvard researchers hit upon evidence that seems to explain this perplexing phenomenon, perhaps finally proving centuries of naysayers wrong. "Acute stress, particularly the fight-or-flight response, has been traditionally viewed to be beneficial for an animal's survival," noted researcher Bing Zhang. But a response system beneficial to our safety and survival may still spur changes in other parts of our body, including our hair. "When we started to study this," explained fellow researcher Ya-Chieh Hsu, "I expected that stress was bad for the body—but the detrimental impact of stress that we discovered was beyond what I imagined."

As summarized by science reporter Katie Spalding, the Harvard researchers "exposed mice to various stressors at different stages of hair growth. With each exposure, the researchers found that the rodents' hair follicles lost the pigment [color]-producing melanocyte stem cells, until eventually the mice were left with patches of Marie Antoinette-esque white fur." Concludes fellow researcher Isaac Chiu, "With this study, we now know that neurons can control stem cells and their function and can explain how they interact at the cellular and molecular levels to link stress with hair-graying."[225]

Shockingly, this whitening process happened quickly. "After just a few days," explains Hsu, "all of the pigment-regenerating stem cells were lost. Once they're gone, you can't regenerate pigments anymore. The damage is permanent." The study's results are certain to have wide-ranging impact. For "by understanding precisely how stress affects stem cells that regenerate pigment, we've laid the groundwork for understanding how stress affects other tissues and organs in the body." And this key understanding in etiology—as to *how* stress works, its causes and consequences—is the critical first step for then discovering and developing possible treatments for blocking and halting the damaging effects of stress.

In the end, therefore, "it may well have been grief that turned Marie Antoinette's hair white after all," concludes Spalding.[226] And likely contributed as well to the famed matronly look of one of the most admired and liked—but mocked and lampooned—First Ladies in American history.

"It may well have been grief that turned Marie Antoinette's hair white after all."

DNA: History's Handmaid

Science is routinely now solving historical mysteries, including long-standing presidential quandaries, and a frequent key to the puzzle solving is that simple, universal, and fundamental life element called hair. Why? Because of hair's abundant nature, durability over time, and rich repository of chemical information, including DNA.

James Breig, writing in *Colonial Williamsburg Journal*, has nicely summarized the kind of impact that science and DNA have had on our understanding of the past:

The methods of knowing about the past took a quantum leap in 1953 with the discovery of DNA, a double helix of a genetic corkscrew historians and genealogists wielded more and more to bore into mysteries and answer old puzzles. Was a Frenchman who died in the nineteenth century really the son of Louis XVI and Marie Antoinette, as he claimed? Non, said DNA. Is Jesse James buried in Jesse James's grave? Reckon so, said DNA. Was a twentieth-century woman, Anastasia, the lost child of Russian royalty? Nyet, said DNA. Who was the infant killed in the sinking of the Titanic and buried as unknown? Eighteen-month-old Sidney Leslie Goodwin of England, said DNA.[227]

But it's not just the dusty, distant past that DNA is elucidating, but very recent history as well, including events affecting the American presidency. In fact, without DNA, President Bill Clinton would likely never have been impeached.

Photograph of President Bill Clinton and White House intern Monica Lewinsky at the White House, February 28, 1997.

As so often happens in Washington, it is commonly not the shenanigans of politicos that get them in trouble but their feeble attempts to cover them up, and that was certainly the case concerning the salacious and scintillating affair between President Clinton and Monica Lewinsky. For Clinton's critical misstep, the one that nearly cost him the presidency, was tied not to philandering and lust but to lying and law. The key moment occurred on January 17, 1998, when Clinton was asked under oath—amid a deposition related to a lawsuit involving a sexual harassment charge leveled against him by Paula Jones, a onetime civil servant in Arkansas, where Clinton was governor—whether he had ever engaged in an extramarital affair with White House intern Monica Lewinsky, who was only twenty-two years old when her liaisons with the president began. "I have never had sexual relations with [her]," Clinton stated. "I have never had an affair with her." He repeated his denial nine days later, with his wife by his side, to a national audience, enunciating sternly what became the most famous line stemming from the scandal. "I did not have sexual relations with that woman, Miss Lewinsky." The next day on *TODAY*, First Lady Hillary Clinton defended her husband and repeated his vow of innocence, denouncing the allegations against him as part of "a vast right-wing conspiracy."[228]

Now, a "vast right-wing conspiracy" may have existed, but it wasn't, as the world soon learned, the source of the president's immediate problems. No, the president had simply lied—to his wife, to the country, to his staff and supporters. In fact, Clinton might have taken the truth to his grave—pulling off the cover-up and limiting the scandal to an embarrassing but likely politically survivable bout of PR ping-pong, "he said, she said"—were it not for the presence of a nearly indisputable witness to his affair with the randy intern: DNA. For unbeknownst to the president, Lewinsky had saved one of the dresses she had worn during their many trysts—and not just any dress, but one stained with the president's semen, no less. After reaching an immunity and cooperation agreement on July 28, protecting herself from any charge of perjury, Lewinsky turned over the soiled navy-blue dress to

No, the president had simply lied—to his wife, to the country, to his staff and supporters.

the investigative office of Independent Counsel Kenneth Starr, who in turned compelled the president to give a blood sample. Comparative analysis of the dress and the blood sample followed, with the results confirmed on August 6: the notorious mess on the dress was Clinton's semen "to a reasonable degree of scientific certainty." As explained in greater detail on August 17, "the genetic markers on the semen, which match the President's DNA, are characteristic of one out of 7.87 trillion Caucasians."[229]

The game was up; Clinton had lied to the American people and lied under oath, and now Congress had the evidence to prove it. On December 19, the US House of Representatives passed two articles of impeachment against him, for perjury and obstruction of justice, though in the trial that followed in the US Senate in January to February 1999, a vote for conviction failed to reach the two-thirds mandate (meaning sixty-seven of the one hundred US senators) for removing the president from office. Clinton, at the time, was just the second US president ever to be impeached, and without the aid of science and DNA, this historic moment in presidential history would likely never have occurred.

THOMAS JEFFERSON AND SALLY HEMINGS

DNA was a busy witness to history in 1998, for another US president, a more critical one in the grand sweep of world history, was also in the crosshairs of science that year. This historic leader, in the words of Pulitzer Prize–winning historian Joseph J. Ellis, was "the dead white male who matters most," and the "most valued trophy in the culture wars": Thomas Jefferson.[230]

As detailed in a bombshell report released at the very time the Clinton-Lewinsky affair was unfolding, there was now scientific evidence to buttress the belief that Jefferson had fathered a child with his slave Sally Hemings, who was beautiful, biracial, very light-skinned, and a half sister to his deceased wife, Martha. This story had long been rumored, dubbed by Ellis "the longest-running miniseries in American history." As the historian noted, "throughout the nineteenth century the 'Tom and Sally' story, as it was then known, persisted as a titillating piece of innuendo that cast a shadow of doubt over Jefferson's reputation in the history books." The rumors and innuendos had even circulated in Jefferson's day. As reported in *The Recorder* of Richmond, Virginia, in 1802 by professional scandalmonger James Callender (who had previously published details about Alexander Hamilton's affair with a married woman),

> It is well known that the man, whom it delight-eth the people to honor, keeps, and for many years past has kept, as his concubine, one of his own slaves. Her name is SALLY. . . . By this wench Sally, our president has had several children.[231]

Amateur poets of the day picked up the story, too, scribbling and circulating doggerel about the president and "Dusky Sally" that only further solidified the story in the public mind. But it was only two centuries later, with advances in DNA analysis—in particular, new methods for tracing male Y chromosomes, which are largely passed unchanged from father to son—that statistically reliable results in such paternity matters were finally possible. Mercifully, the clarifying light of science could now be cast on this two-hundred-year-old story.

What followed sent shockwaves through the academic world. "The results revealed a perfect match between specific portions of Jefferson's Y chromosome and the Y chromosome of Eston [Sally's last son] Hemings (born 1808)," noted Ellis. "The chance of such a match occurring in a random sample is less than one in a thousand."[232] The timing of this blockbuster study was highly suspicious to Conservative conspiratorialists. From their perspective, a left-leaning scientific community had conveniently come to Clinton's rescue, trying to mitigate the president's impeachable offenses by showing the White House precedence for such sexual incontinence.

> *"The chance of such a match occurring in a random sample is less than one in a thousand."*

Circumstantial evidence from history, however, had long supported the DNA results. First, the father of Sally's children was obviously a light-skinned man, given their own light complexion (in fact, several of her children socially passed as white), and their features were strikingly similar to Jefferson's. Plus, we know that the timing of Sally's pregnancies coincided with periods when Jefferson was present, either at his home at Monticello in Virginia, where Sally served as a house slave, or in Paris, where Sally was a body servant to his daughter and a maid in Jefferson's household while he served as minister to France, militating against the likelihood that other males in the extended Jefferson family with the same Y chromosome could have fathered her children—they just didn't have the same proximity and access to Sally that Thomas repeatedly did. Moreover, Sally's son Madison, in an 1873 memoir, outright confirmed the decades-long liaisons between the president and his mother, revealing details of the "treaty" that supposedly arose between them:

My mother accompanied [Thomas's daughter, to Paris] as her body servant. . . . During that time my mother became Mr. Jefferson's concubine, and when he was called home she was *enciente* [pregnant] by him. He desired to bring my mother back to Virginia with him but she demurred. She was just beginning to understand the French language well, and in France she was free, while if she returned to Virginia she would be re-enslaved. So she refused to return with him. To induce her to do so he promised her extraordinary privileges, and made a solemn pledge that her children should be freed at the age of twenty-one years. In consequence of his promises, on which she implicitly relied, she returned with him to Virginia. Soon after their arrival, she gave birth to a child, of whom Thomas Jefferson was the father. It lived but a short time. She gave birth to four others, and Jefferson was the father of all of them. Their names were Beverly, Harriet, Madison (myself), and Eston—three sons and one daughter. We all became free agreeably to the treaty entered into by our parents before we were born.[233]

Although most observers today agree, as stated by the Thomas Jefferson Foundation, "that the issue [of a sexual relationship between Jefferson and Hemings that resulted in at least one child, if not all of Sally's children] is a settled historical matter," the *nature* of their relationship—how to characterize the widowed Jefferson's paternity and affair with his slave—is far from settled. Science can help us with the *what* and the *when* concerning something that happened, and maybe also with the *how*, but discovering *why* something occurred can be far more problematic.

For was their relationship based on deep attraction and love, especially since Sally likely shared features with the president's beloved deceased wife, Martha, who was also Sally's half sister? Unfortunately, there are no photographs or painted portraits of Sally—only a couple of written descriptions of her. The president's eldest grandson, Thomas Jefferson Randolph, remembered her as "light colored and decidedly good looking," and she was known around the Jefferson plantation as "Dashing Sally." Slave Isaac Jefferson concurred, recording she was "mighty near white . . . very handsome." And what was one of Dashing Sally's most distinguishing features, according to Isaac? Her "long straight hair down her back."[234]

MARTHA JEFFERSON

Interestingly, there are no known portraits or paintings of Martha Jefferson either, and as with Sally, there are few descriptions of her looks. Doubly interesting, among the scant verbal sketches of Martha that do exist, it's clear that both she and her half sister, Sally, shared a singular attribute: gorgeous hair. "Beautiful, musical, well read, and intelligent, she [Martha] was five and a half years younger than Jefferson," noted Henry S. Randall, one of Jefferson's earliest biographers, whose description of Martha was based on firsthand interviews with the president's immediate family. "Her complexion was brilliant—her large expressive eyes of the richest shade of hazel," and her hair was "luxuriant" and "of the finest tinge of auburn," mirroring Thomas's "reddish chestnut hair," which was equally "luxuriant and silken."[235] In fact, Jefferson cherished his wife's hair even after her death in September 1782.

Jefferson cherished his wife's hair even after her death in September 1782.

Suffering from the strain of multiple pregnancies, Martha never recovered from the birth, in May 1782, of their last daughter, Lucy, beginning a four-month decline in Martha's health. During this period, Thomas was emotionally wrought and rarely left his wife's side as she struggled to survive. "He was never out of calling," noted their eldest daughter, Martha. "When not at her bedside, he was writing in a small room which opened immediately at the head of her bed. A moment before the closing [death] scene, he was led from the room almost in a state of insensibility by his sister Mrs. Carr, who, with great difficulty, got him into his library, where he fainted."[236]

But Martha didn't die before extracting an important promise from Thomas. From her deathbed, as she struggled to breathe her final breaths, Martha made him promise he would never remarry, for she "could not die happy if she thought her . . . children were ever to have a stepmother brought in over them."[237] Thomas promised, and he kept his word. He also, immediately upon her death, did something else in honor of Martha, and it involved her hair. As Martin Dugard and Bill O'Reilly recount in *Killing England: The Brutal Struggle for American Independence* (2017),

> As Thomas Jefferson begins the process of burning all her letters to protect forever the privacy of their love from the world, he wraps this last piece of her handwriting [transcribing a verse about the fleeting nature of time and our brief time to love, from Laurence Sterne's novel *Tristram Shandy*] in a lock of her hair and hides it in his writing desk, so that Martha will always be with him.[238]

When Jefferson died forty-four years later, this hair and handwritten note by Martha, along with other mementos of their children, were discovered in envelopes, notes Randall, "arranged in perfect order," all labeled "in [Thomas's] own hand," and stored in "the most secret drawer of a private cabinet which he constantly resorted to." But the hair and mementos were not mere historic relics stored for posterity—they were intimate, living elements of Thomas's life. For the physical condition of the envelopes, adds Randall, "indicated their frequent handling."[239] During the next two years after Martha's death, the grief-stricken Jefferson withdrew from public life. "For ills so immense," he wrote, "time and silence are the only medicines."[240]

MARIA COSWAY: THOMAS HAD A TYPE

Family and friends who cared about Jefferson, however, thought differently, and they urged a change in geography for mitigating his woe. He finally consented, accepting the position as US minister to France in 1784 and relocating to Paris. There, two years later, the widowed diplomat fell madly in love . . . with a married woman; she was twenty-seven, he forty-three. He was introduced to her by famed artist John Trumbull, known as "The Painter of the Revolution," and the affair that ensued could have derailed his political career, if not ruined his opportunity ever to become president.

Confident and assertive, vivacious and striking in every way, with qualities both angelic and alluring, this enchantress was a kind of distaff doppelgänger of Jefferson the Renaissance Man, mirroring in her wide-ranging talents and triumphs the very encyclopedic abilities of Thomas himself. She spoke several languages, in a soft and seductive, lilting way; sang like a nightingale; discoursed like a scholar on art and architecture; mastered the harp, the harpsichord, and the organ; produced paintings and engravings owned today by the British Library, British Museum, and New York Public Library, and exhibited recently at London's National Portrait Gallery and Tate Britain; founded a Catholic girl's school as well as a convent (in her youth, she had nearly become

Maria Cecilia Louisa Cosway, by Valentine Green, 1787.

a nun); and possessed such grace, eloquence, wit, and uncanny beauty that men melted before her.

Jefferson certainly did, even breaking his right wrist on one occasion while either showing off for her by trying to jump a fence or misjudging his leap over a small decorative pool and fountain on his giddy run to his carriage for a rendezvous with her. He followed up the embarrassing mishap with a maudlin four-thousand-word love letter to her, the only love letter extant among his voluminous correspondence, in which his Heart battles in dialogue with his Head over the propriety and prudence of their relationship.

Interestingly, Jefferson had to write the lengthy love letter with his non-dominant left hand, since his right wrist was still impaired from the accident, but he did so with extraordinary deft and clarity. (The multitalented and multilingual president James Garfield also possessed this ambidextrous talent—he could reportedly write a sentence in Greek with one hand while simultaneously composing the same line in Latin with the other hand.)

As one writer cleverly described Jefferson's new, married love interest,

> Maria Louisa Caterina Cecilia Hadfield Cosway was such a total package of sexiness and brilliance that she needed six names. With eyes as blue as violets . . . a slim figure, and (according to Jefferson biographer Dumas Malone) "kissable" pouting lips, Maria Cosway was the perfect femme fatale.[241]

"Maria Louisa Caterina Cecilia Hadfield Cosway was such a total package of sexiness and brilliance that she needed six names."

And one additional feature she exhibited was impossible to overlook, a feature enjoyed by both Sally Hemings and Martha Jefferson: striking hair. In Cosway's case, gorgeous, curly golden locks. It seems, when it came to women, Thomas "had a type."

Despite the striking physical traits shared by all three women, there was a stark difference in the case of Sally Hemings, which begs the question: If Sally and Tom's relationship was not based on mutual attraction, affection, and love, was it founded instead on power and privilege? After all, Sally was likely only fourteen years old when their relationship began, and he was thirty years her senior—and her master, no less; in other words, Jefferson legally owned her and her body.

Although it's tempting to judge historic characters outside their time and place, exposing their reputations (unfairly) to the whims and ways of the present, Jefferson's relationship with Hemings is nonetheless troubling, raising ethical questions tied to age, consent, power, and ownership that may or may not be mitigated by the mores of their time.

So, in the end, what to make of all this? How do the revelations garnered from science and DNA impact our perception of Jefferson, enslaver of more than six hundred men, women, and children in his lifetime; one of the most significant of the Founding Fathers; and one of the world's most eloquent voices on behalf of liberty, who penned what is likely the most consequential line in history, "All men are created equal"? After all, we live daily with Jefferson. His name adorns countless cities, counties, schools, and streets; his face graces our coins and currency; and he gazes down on us from the heights of Mount Rushmore and through the majestic colonnade of his memorial in Washington, DC. Given all this, does this giant of American history—lo, *world* history—remain a hero in our eyes, or is he a hypocrite instead? Or measures of both? Or could he even be considered, as his sharpest critics charge, a pedophile rapist?

Although there will never again be a consensus on this question of Jefferson's character—indeed, the once marmoreal reputation of the Founding Fathers is clearly no longer fixed and unmalleable, with their splendid achievements as well as colossal failures now in high relief—science and DNA

> *Science and DNA have likely confirmed for all time . . . Jefferson's paternal role in a complicated and controversial affair of history.*

have likely confirmed for all time at least two fundamental facts about the remarkable third US president: Jefferson's paternal role in a complicated and controversial affair of history, and his status as a man of mighty contradictions—a paragon of Churchill's famed riddle, wrapped in a mystery, inside an enigma.

WARREN G. HARDING, LADIES' MAN

New advances in science and technology are clearly spurring a revision of our history books, especially the chapters on the private, domestic lives of the presidents. The long-lingering paternity matter shadowing the life and legacy of Warren G. Harding (29th US president, 1921–23) is yet another example.

Although not widely considered an Adonis today, the hairy-browed Harding was distinguished looking nonetheless, in a sober and serious way, and he was devilishly handsome to the women of his day. He had an easy way with the ladies, and at least two extramarital affairs, including a steamy one that lasted for years with a fetching young blonde secretary, Nan Britton; she was thirty years his junior and barely out of high school when their liaisons began. Four years after the president died in 1923, Britton published what many have called the first presidential kiss-and-tell book, *The President's Daughter* (1927), a publication that scandalized the nation. A book about illicit sex was a perfect fit for an era giddy on gin, jazz, and frivolity, and it became a bestseller—it was even sold door-to-door, concealed in brown paper.

Britton addressed the purpose of her book in its first pages. "If love is the only right warrant for bringing children into the world," she asserted, "then many children born in wedlock are illegitimate and many born out of wedlock are legitimate." Her motive, she claimed, was not pernicious or greedily parasitic but grounded in "the need for legal and social recognition and protection of all children in these United States born out of wedlock." Britton then revealed, in steamy detail, her abiding love for the president, exposing in the process their six-and-a-half-year affair, their discussion of a possible abortion

(whether she would do it with strong medicine or via an operation, "he personally would prefer 'the knife,'" she claimed about the president), and even their heated, carnal encounters in a White House coat closet.[242]

Proclaiming Harding as the father of her daughter, Elizabeth Ann Blaesing (born in 1919), Britton was vilified by the press and the Harding family alike as a liar, a gold digger, a degenerate, and a pervert. Britton said Harding had privately acknowledged his paternity and even provided monthly support for her financially (payments kindly hand delivered by the Secret Service), but he never admitted this publicly, and she went to her grave in 1991 still professing the truth of her story.

Unrelenting were the seventy years of ridicule she experienced in the interim, which lawyer and writer James Robenalt, author of *The Harding Affair: Love and Espionage during the Great War* (2009)—a book about Harding's earlier affair with a woman named Carrie Phillips—compared to the shaming experienced by yet another young inamorata of yet another US president, Bill Clinton. "Nan Britton was someone who had to live through a lot of attacks . . . and I think her story was a lot like Monica Lewinsky because there was a real shaming process."[243]

Science, as demonstrated by the leading role that DNA had played in the Clinton and Jefferson affairs, obviously held the key to solving this matter concerning Britton and the president, and the path toward a paternity test began in earnest after Harding's grandnephew, Dr. Peter Harding, a former Navy psychiatrist, noticed similarities between Britton's relationship with the president and details surrounding Harding's earlier affair with Phillips.

Warren G. Harding, photographed by Harris & Ewing, circa 1920.

As Peter Harding told me in a phone interview, he noticed a pattern in the president's affair with Phillips and in the passions expressed in their love letters that mirrored the events and emotions related in Nan Britton's tell-all work. (Philanderers are creatures of habit, even in their prose.) In fact, many of Britton's claims can be corroborated in the president's earlier letters to Phillips. Nonetheless, as Peter explained, the Harding family had long considered Britton "a delusional woman who believed in a fantasy," because Warren Harding had been considered infertile due to a childhood bout with the mumps; he had fathered no children with his wife, Florence, the First Lady. But the Nan Britton story wouldn't go away. "It [was] Shakespearean and operatic," said Peter to the *New York Times*; it hung "over the whole [of] presidential history because it was an unsolved mystery."[244] Moreover, this rumored second affair seemed highly plausible to Peter. As a medical professional and a trained psychiatrist, "I know 'delusional,'" he told me, and "there was nothing in Britton's book about the affair that sounded crazy or made up."

So, wanting definitive proof to settle this matter once and for all, Peter contacted James Blaesing, the reported son of Harding and Britton's love child, but he did so with trepidation. "Each family has their own set of beliefs," explained Peter. "We both broke with our family ideology, and I feared losing friendships within the family. I was violating a lot of family rules to bring this about." But Blaesing gladly cooperated with Peter. "I wanted to prove who she [my mother] was and prove everyone wrong."[245]

DNA testing followed in 2015, courtesy of Ancestry.com, leading to genetic evidence that finally ended this decades-long contretemps: the analysis showed that Peter and James were second cousins, which meant President Harding was indeed the father of Elizabeth Ann Blaesing, James's mother, and that Nan Britton, James's grandmother, had indeed been telling the truth all along about her affair with the president. Thanks to science, Nan Britton and her family had finally been vindicated.

Thanks to science, Nan Britton and her family had finally been vindicated.

HARDING'S RACIAL HERITAGE

The DNA results in this case also *dis*proved another mystery swirling around Warren Harding—whether he, and not Barack Obama, deserved the sobriquet as the first African American president in US history. This long-lingering rumor—that Harding's heritage included "Black blood"—had been fueled by Harding himself, when he once told a reporter, rather inelegantly, that "one of [his] ancestors may have jumped the fence."[246]

White racist Democratic opponents of Harding, who was a Republican, frequently played this race card against him, offering it as proof, ipso facto, of his unsuitability for political office. Racist whites, in fact, had good reason to fear Harding, not because of his blood, but because of his beliefs—despite his popular ranking as one of the worst presidents in American history, Harding was a courageous and early crusader for equal rights for women and Blacks alike, supporting suffrage for the former and an antilynching law for the latter.

But this suspicion about Harding's "African American heritage" lingered for decades, alongside the very mystery surrounding his affair with Nan Britton. As reported by the *New York Times*, when the president's grandniece, Abigail Harding, was a baby in the 1940s, a random woman on the street once stopped and peeked in her carriage, just "to see if she was Black." But the DNA analysis performed in the 2015 paternity case finally put to rest this mystery as well: there were no "detectable genetic signatures of sub-Saharan African heritage," reported Ancestry.com.[247]

HAIR SCIENCE

Science is clearly solving innumerable historical mysteries, especially those tied to questions of paternity, ancestry, and race. But science is also clarifying how several US presidents died, and a frequent key to these revelations is that common element of uncommon power: hair.

Because of hair's durability and stability over time, and its capacity for capturing long-term information about our health and drug use, hair as a biomarker is a godsend in diagnostic and forensic medicine. It's useful to doctors monitoring the effect of prescribed drugs, veterinarians treating ill animals, detectives and medical examiners analyzing crimes, and even professional sports associations screening for illegal doping. It's also a key component of anthropological and archaeometric research today, providing scholars with keen insights into ancient civilizations—about how people lived, their quality of life, their diet, how far they traveled, and how they died—all from analysis of the chemical treasures hidden safely away in the hair and DNA of mummies thousands of years old. Because of hair's steady growth rate, it can even provide a chronological snapshot of elements once circulating in the blood.

Because of hair's steady growth rate, it can even provide a chronological snapshot of elements once circulating in the blood.

Hair's extraordinary abilities were front and center in the controversy surrounding Zachary Taylor (12th US president, 1849–50). The question was simple, but shocking: *Was Taylor—and not Abraham Lincoln—the first president assassinated in American history?*

ZACHARY TAYLOR'S QUICK AND PUZZLING DEATH

Taylor's life was crowned and crowded with great glory and success, but nearly all of it occurred *before* he reached the White House, and nearly all of it happened on the battlefield. Valiantly he had served in every major military campaign in the country's history between the Revolutionary War and the Civil War: the War of 1812–15, the Black Hawk War of 1832, the Second

Seminole War of 1832–42, and the Mexican-American War of 1846–48 (in the seminal Battle of Buena Vista in particular, when he rallied his men against an enemy treble the size of his forces). Taylor served fearlessly in each, displaying exceptional coolness and courage under fire. He led not from behind but alongside his men, often engaging in bloody hand-to-hand combat, earning their great respect ("Old Rough-and-Ready," they affectionately christened him). He also garnered wide press attention that made him a national hero—although few Americans remember Taylor today, and few could list him as an American president, he was the Eisenhower and MacArthur of his day.[248]

His four decades of national service and commitment to the Union appealed to Northerners, while his Southern roots and status as a wealthy slave owner reassured Southerners, thereby pleasing enough folks on both sides of the political aisle to pave a path of popularity that led to the White House and his victory in the election of 1848. But despite his electoral success, Taylor possessed neither the training nor temperament to be a successful president.

Homespun and inelegant in speech and manner and never a deep thinker, with few political bones in his body and even fewer political positions of any great clarity and conviction, he was a soldier to the core, accustomed to battlefield loyalty, unthinking selflessness, and clear-cut command—not the paltering, jobbery, and general rascality so common in the back halls of high-stakes politics. In fact, he was the first president ever elected who had never previously held political office of any kind, and until his own campaign for the presidency, he had never even voted in an election.

This was hardly a propitious time in American history for a political neophyte, when partisanship was at a fever pitch and the stakes over the Union were never

Zachary Taylor, oil on canvas, painted by artist Joseph Henry Bush, 1848.

higher. Taylor himself said that "no sane person" would ever consider him presidential material, and historians have largely agreed with his self-assessment. "Most historians believe that he was too nonpolitical in a day when politics, parties, and presidential leadership demanded close ties with political operatives," writes historian Michael Holt.[249]

Unsurprisingly, his public acclaim and nonpartisan appeal notwithstanding, his presidency was a disaster, beset with conflict and controversy, including sectional strife, endless debates over slavery and its extension to new territories, and scandals involving financial skullduggery among members of his cabinet.

Arguably, the most notable event to occur during his presidency was his death—after only sixteen months in office—an event, ironically, that did more to unify the country, in common grief, than perhaps any of the president's policies.

"No sane person" would ever consider him presidential material, and historians have largely agreed with his self-assessment.

DEATH BY DEADLY FRUIT?

When Taylor died on July 9, 1850, he became only the second president to die in office—but *how* did he die? Key to his demise were the events of July 4, five days earlier, when the president celebrated Independence Day.

It was one of those typical summertime DC days—oppressively hot and humid—and before or after attending a Sunday school recital that morning, the president cooled off by eating several green apples. In the afternoon, he attended a ceremony at the recently begun Washington Monument, where he sat in the scorching sun, bareheaded, listening to orations; to stay hydrated, he drank several glasses of water. After the ceremony, the hot and perspiring president, perhaps suffering the effects of mild heatstroke, ambled along the Potomac River for a spell before returning to the White House, where he attempted to cool off once more and revive his energy by downing a large quantity of iced milk, a large bowl of fruit (likely cherries), and some raw vegetables.[250]

Within hours, the president was doubled over in pain, suffering intense cramps and diarrhea. His condition worsened the following day, as he suffered chest pains, fever, vomiting, and dehydration. Worried doctors quickly prescribed a series of drugs: opium (for pain relief), calomel (a dangerous mercury compound and laxative), and quinine (to quash the fever). When nothing worked, the doctors resorted to that centuries-old solution to nearly any mysterious ailment—bloodletting, as well as a bout of blistering of the skin using hot plasters, which was believed to relieve fevers. These attempted "cures" merely hastened the president's decline, and on the morning of July 9, the president himself realized the end was near. "I am not afraid to die; I expect the summons soon; I have endeavored to discharge all of my official duties faithfully; I regret nothing; but I am sorry that I am about to leave my friends,"[251] he muttered from his bed to loved ones gathered around him. The president died that evening.

According to Dr. Allan B. Schwartz, what killed the president was a combination of factors, both environmental and medical:

> "I am not afraid to die; I expect the summons soon; . . . I regret nothing; but I am sorry that I am about to leave my friends."

After Taylor's death, it was discovered that the water supply of Washington was contaminated by sewage that flowed into a marsh not far from the White House. This marsh provided an environment for salmonella bacteria and other organisms capable of causing typhoid fever and paratyphoid fever. There was no typhoid vaccine protection or antibiotic treatments as there are today.

Whatever the source of infection, the hot weather and Washington's open, fly-infested sewers undoubtedly aggravated the situation. And Taylor's fate was probably sealed by his doctor's ill-conceived "treatments" of bleeding and calomel, a purgative, which worsened diarrhea and vomiting.[252]

So, DC's horrible sanitation situation (which likely also caused the death of President William Henry Harrison in 1841 and the death of Lincoln's eleven-year-old son, Willie, in 1862), in combination with the doctors' dubious treatments, probably sealed the president's fate. The exact medical condition that killed Taylor, according to most historians and medical experts today, was "acute gastroenteritis." In Taylor's day, this condition was diagnosed as *cholera morbus*, a convenient catchall finding frequently ascribed in the nineteenth century to mysterious ailments of many sorts.

THE ASSASSINATION THEORY

But had Taylor really died this way? From natural causes stemming from dangerous environmental elements and primitive medical practices? Or had the president instead, intentionally and with malice aforethought, been *murdered*?

Such was the shocking suggestion of one Clara Rising, a retired professor of humanities at the University of Florida. Like any good sleuth, to prove such an act, Rising needed evidence of the three main pillars of crime—motive, means, and opportunity—and by 1990, the professor was certain she had hit the jackpot and amassed evidence of all three.

After all, in the days leading up to his death, Taylor had pushed for expedited statehood for both California and New Mexico, areas likely to enter the Union as *free* states; this would upset the precarious balance of free and slave states and tip the scale in favor of the former. Therefore, from Rising's perspective, there were plenty of Southerners for whom the unforeseen death of a Northern-sympathizing president would not have been an entirely unwelcome development. Such was the *motive*. Rising also saw plenty of *opportunity* for murdering the president. "The White House in those days had no FBI, no Secret Service," she explained on C-SPAN. "Mrs. Taylor [the First Lady] often complained that there were strangers wandering around in the bedrooms." This left only *means*, and for this Rising lighted on one of the most popular and pervasive substances of the nineteenth century: *arsenic*. The ubiquity back then of this odorless, colorless, and ever-so-dangerous metalloid is impossible to overstate. Beer, wine, candy, clothing, cosmetics, candles, soap, paints, toys, wallpaper, insecticides—arsenic and arsenic-based pigments seemed to be a component of everything, everywhere. It was even a common element in the medicines of the day, prescribed to treat fevers, asthma, syphilis, diabetes, psoriasis, and ulcers, among other ailments. In fact, arsenic continues to be prescribed today, in certain treatments for certain diseases.[253]

But that which can cure can also kill, and arsenic is perfectly constituted to do both.

But that which can cure can also kill, and arsenic is perfectly constituted to do both. As Joan Acocella wrote in "Murder by Poison,"

> In early nineteenth-century England, a good way to get rid of your husband was arsenic. A medical examiner usually couldn't tell whether the poison was involved, because the symptoms—diarrhea, vomiting, abdominal pain—are much like those of other disorders. Nor could he necessarily place you at the murder scene. The dying typically took hours. Also, you could administer the poison gradually, a little bit every day. In the mid-century, arsenic poisoning was commonly the resort of women.[254]

But two characteristics of arsenic have had a special appeal to the murderous minded. "The great attraction of arsenious acid to those contemplating murder is that it has no distinctive taste or smell," explained James C. Whorton in *The Arsenic Century: How Victorian Britain Was Poisoned at Home, Work, and Play* (2010), "and since it resembles flour and sugar, [it] can be added to foods and beverages without amassing suspicion."[255] Hence the obsession with arsenic among crime writers the world over.

What especially intrigued Rising was the similarity of the symptoms suffered by the president and those commonly associated with arsenic poisoning. Nausea, diarrhea, vomiting, weakness, abdominal pain, fever—these symptoms of poisoning mirror the very conditions experienced by the president during those critical final five days of his life in early July 1850. However, to prove arsenic poisoning, Rising needed to show not only that arsenic was present in the president's body—a fact that would hardly have been surprising, given the ubiquity of the substance in the nineteenth century—but that it existed in elevated and sufficient quantities to kill him. And to prove this, Rising turned to that simple, universal, and fundamental life element called *hair*.

To glean any such insights in the Zachary Taylor case, Rising would need a sample of the president's plumage—from a man who had died more than a century

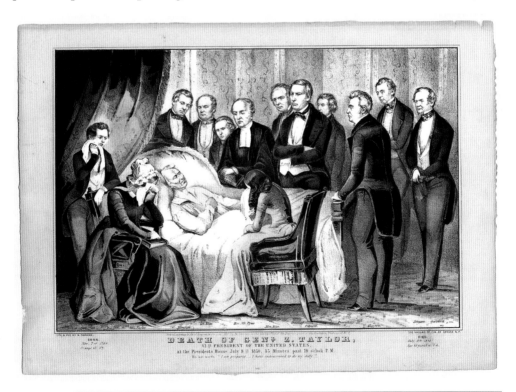

President Zachary Taylor on his death bed in the White House, July 1850; Currier lithograph, 1850.

ago. Rising found two sources of hair samples: one from the Smithsonian Institution and the other in New Orleans. Unfortunately, both samples proved useless—the first one had been contaminated by pesticides, and the latter proved to be not from Taylor but from "Old Hickory," the "Hero of New Orleans," Andrew Jackson.

With nowhere else to turn, Rising decided to go to the source itself, Taylor's entombed body; she would seek permission to have the president disinterred. To do this, Rising needed the approval of a Taylor relative, and she found it in an eighty-four-year-old distant grandson of the president. With his permission secured, Rising then petitioned the coroner in Jefferson County, Kentucky, where the president was buried, and he in turn sought the blessing of the Department of Veterans Affairs, administrator of the Zachary Taylor National Cemetery.

Astonishingly, especially to historians who had dismissed Rising's assassination theory as ludicrous, the professor secured all the permissions for disinterring the president, and on June 17, 1991, the president's body was removed from its dusty crypt in Louisville, Kentucky, and transported by hearse to the local coroner's laboratory. Opening the timeworn casket proved difficult, and only with the assistance of power tools could the coffin finally be cracked. But once "we finally got the lid off," recounted Kentucky State Medical Examiner George Nichols, "there were Zachary Taylor's fully dressed remains. I'd never met a president before . . . he didn't offer much in the way of conversation."[256]

Regarding that comma of hair on the forehead so often depicted in portraits of the president, it was now missing.

Although the president was "dried out like a sponge" and his skin "seriously leathered," it was possible to acquire the desired anatomical samples: hair—from the president's head, sideburns, and even pubic region—as well as nails from all ten fingers. Regarding that comma of hair on the forehead so often depicted in portraits of the president, it was now missing, noted Rising. "All the portraits showed a man with sandy-colored hair," she later wrote, "tending to curl, one unruly lock falling onto his forehead, giving to that weathered face a certain boyish look. Even when his hair was white this lock stuck out, refusing to be tamed. It was gone now." The president's teeth, however, were present and pristine, facilitating dental analysis. Writer Zachary Crockett has nicely summarized the various high-tech methods used for analyzing the samples:

> To test for the arsenic, Nichols collected various dental, bone, and hair samples, and sent them to three different facilities: The first batch went to the State Toxicology Laboratory, where it was tested using colorimetric analysis (the use of a color agent to detect trace elements). A second batch went to the University of Louisville to be scanned with an electron microscope equipped with X-ray diffraction analysis (allowing for close-up molecular views of the follicles). The final batch accompanied Nichols on an airplane to Oak Ridge National Lab for neutron activation analysis, a fairly new technique in which a sample is "bombarded with neutrons, causing the elements to form radioactive isotopes."[257]

The analysis of the samples took only weeks, whereupon the verdict was released to the public and the press: the level of arsenic in the president's body was hundreds of times lower than the quantity needed to kill him. Although "the symptoms [the president] exhibited and the rapidity of his death are clearly consistent with acute arsenic poisoning," stated Nichols in his written report, "it is my opinion that Zachary Taylor died as the result of one of a myriad of natural diseases which would have produced the symptoms of gastroenteritis"—in other words, the exact medical condition and diagnosis long cited by historians and medical experts. "Final Opinion," concluded Nichols: "The manner of death is natural."[258]

Lincoln's status as the first president assassinated in American history remains secure.

The media raked Professor Rising over the proverbial coals. An editorial in the *New York Times* not only castigated her for a pointless exercise but also accused her of sacrilege. "Sometimes there are good reasons for tampering with a grave," it argued, and "serious historical evidence establishing the possibility that President Taylor was assassinated would be one. But Ms. Rising has produced no such evidence, only a hypothesis. . . . All that's been revealed . . . is a cavalier contempt for the dead."[259]

AMERICA'S LAST KING

Actually, something else was clearly revealed and reinforced in the Taylor case, a lesson larger and more meaningful than solving a single presidential mystery: the important role that science, technology, and hair can now play in clarifying and correcting our understanding of history.

This point was underscored in 2005, when hair analysis of another world leader—most significantly, of the one man in a position to prevent the formation of the American presidency in the first place—proved the very opposite of the conclusion reached in the Taylor case: that high levels of arsenic in the body of this earlier leader likely *had* affected his health and ability to discharge his public duties. The leader in question? America's last king, England's King George III.

For many folks today, King George is first and foremost that bumbling and babbling scene-stealer in the hit musical *Hamilton*. But the king was actually one of the longest-serving monarchs in English history (serving nearly sixty years) and far from the awful tyrant portrayed by the Founding Fathers and in the musical. He was, most significantly, the historic leader who lost two seminal things: the American colonies, and his mind. In fact, it was shortly after losing the former that the latter began to manifest itself in increasingly pronounced ways.

Although the king's first significant psychotic episode occurred prewar, in 1765, his postwar afflictions were far worse. The episode lasting from October 1788 to February 1789 was most disturbing, characterized by incessant talking (once nonstop for nineteen hours, often incoherently); frequently foaming at the mouth (on one occasion in January 1812, he would speak for twenty-four hours straight); verbally lashing out at attendants, and sometimes

King George III in Coronation Robes, oil on canvas, painted by artist Allan Ramsay, circa 1765.

striking them; laughing and then weeping uncontrollably; hiding under a sofa; wearing a pillowcase on his head; and even talking to his pillow and referring to himself in the past tense, as "the late King"—"He was a good man." In fact, this period of insanity was so trying on the king's wife that she experienced the same follicle fate as Marie Antoinette and Barbara Bush. "Queen Charlotte's hair turned entirely gray in these months of constant crisis," writes historian Andrew Roberts.[260]

> "Queen Charlotte's hair turned entirely gray in these months of constant crisis."

During these manic states, the king would obsessively roll up and unroll handkerchiefs, button and unbutton his clothes, take apart and reassemble watches, and recite Latin—all repetitive actions that had a calming influence on him, serving as a kind of behavioral therapy. But when out of control, the king was gagged, forced into a straitjacket, and chained to a chair, with his legs bound together. He then endured the wide array of barbaric medical "cures" of his day, including intentional blistering, "cupping" with burning-hot glass vessels, leeches on his temples, and, of course, the perennial favorite, outright bloodletting.

Serious psychotic episodes followed in 1801 and 1804, and by 1812, dementia had reared its ugly head as well, stealing the king's sanity for good; if these developments were not tragic enough, George's vision and hearing soon abandoned him too, leaving him blind, deaf, and mad for the remaining years of his life, until his death (mercifully) in 1820, at the age of eighty-one.

What exactly caused King George's illness has long been debated by scholars and "experts" of one sort or another. One biographer wondered "whether or not it was the blight of God" responsible for the king's illness, while another targeted "the strain of having to make love to his unattractive wife, Queen Charlotte."[261] But in recent decades, specific medical maladies have been suggested as the cause of the king's illness. "From the mid-1960s until 2010," writes Roberts, "it was generally believed that 'the King's malady' from which George III suffered in 1765, 1788–9, 1801, 1804, and 1810–20 was the inherited metabolic disorder porphyria," which resulted in an accumulation of toxins in the king's system.[262] This was the disease promulgated in the popular play *The Madness of George III* (1991) and the subsequent film based on the play, *The Madness of King George* (1994).

According to the Mayo Clinic, acute porphyria can "cause nervous system symptoms, which appear quickly and can be severe," and "symptoms may last days to weeks" and include: severe abdominal pain; pain in your chest, legs, or back; constipation or diarrhea; nausea and vomiting; muscle pain, tingling, numbness, weakness, or paralysis; red or brown urine; mental changes, such as anxiety, confusion, hallucinations, disorientation, or paranoia; breathing problems; urination problems; rapid or irregular heartbeats (palpitations); high blood pressure; and seizures.[263] The king indeed suffered from many of these ailments.

Buttressing the porphyria theory was analysis of the king's hair. As mentioned earlier, King George's powdered perukes, ermine robes, and pearl- and diamond-encrusted crowns of gold had stood him in stark contrast to his relatively unpretentious American counterpart, George Washington, the wigless leader of the upstart Americans during the American Revolution.

And it's here, among the ostentatious dress and mannerisms of the English monarch, that we uncover a key unlocking a keen insight into the king's illness and growing instability. For in 2005 some strands of the king's hair, often hidden in his day by his wigs, were discovered in a vault of the Science Museum in London, and when tested, the hair revealed very high levels of arsenic, a chemical element capable of triggering a genetic predisposition to porphyria. According

Queen Charlotte of England, shown here with her gray hair, oil on canvas, painted by Thomas Gainsborough, 1781.

And it's here . . . that we uncover a key unlocking a keen insight into the king's illness and growing instability.

to one report, the level of arsenic in the king's hair sample was not just elevated but "seventeen times what is believed to be the threshold for arsenic poisoning."[264]

It seems, as part of their treatment of the king's illness, the royal doctors gave the monarch regular doses of an antimony-based emetic to spur vomiting, hoping the purging and cleansing of the king's system would help ease his frequent abdominal pains. But antimony extracted back then was nearly always contaminated with arsenic, and so the doctors' daily cure was likely making the king worse by increasing the levels of arsenic in his system, which in turn had the potential of triggering the increasingly severe bouts of instability that the doctors were hoping to control in the first place; this could well have contributed to the severity of the attacks that the king experienced later in life. But one other item in daily contact with the king also contained arsenic, albeit at lower

A lock of hair from King George III, photographed by the Wellcome Library in London.

levels than the king's daily "medicine": his wigs.[265] Arsenic was a common component in the powder used to whiten the king's perukes as well as natural hair.

As Gertrude Stein reportedly quipped about the bizarre death of dancer Isadora Duncan, whose long silk scarf was blown into a rear wheel of her open car and strangled her to death, "Affectations can be dangerous."

Many scholars today, such as Andrew Roberts, now believe the "king's malady" was not porphyria but bipolarism. However, not everyone agrees, including British biochemist Martin Warren, who's spent years researching the "king's malady." As Warren told me in 2022,

> Not everyone is convinced by the bipolar diagnosis. It is a possibility based on the information provided, but so is the porphyria hypothesis. Both should be considered on their merits. When dealing with retrospective diagnosis, achieving scientific certainty is difficult because of the limited information available in comparison to the way conditions are defined nowadays. In terms of the porphyria hypothesis, there is strong evidence that the condition was present within the Royal Family, but I would agree that the diagnosis of porphyria in George III is not certain. I favor porphyria as an explanation for the King's malady as it is consistent with several behavioral issues, and when reading the medical notes in Windsor you get a real flavor of the King's condition.[266]

And what about the role of arsenic in all this? "Arsenic is also known to push porphyric patients into a worse state," said Warren, and "this level [of arsenic found in the king's system and hair] is way above anything we [scientists] were expecting—it's taken us completely by surprise."[267]

So, regardless of the ultimate nature of the king's malady, whether porphyria or bipolarism, the very high levels of arsenic in his system would likely have exacerbated his physical, cognitive, and psychological disabilities. On this fact most experts concur, and we have hair and science to thank for this insight.

We have hair and science to thank for this insight.

Presidential Hair, Science, and Medicine: Three Final Cases

Hair, science, medicine, and the presidents have intersected numerous times in American history, beyond the few incidents discussed in this chapter, and some of the other examples warrant at least a brief mention here, such as:

The case of Andrew Jackson (7th US president, 1829–37), whom many historians long believed died of mercury and lead poisoning, from bullets in his body due to the many duels he fought and from the medications he took for an array of ailments. Two samples of his hair—one from 1815 and another from 1839—were tested in 1999, and while the hair reflected "significantly elevated" levels of both substances, they were not, according to the American Medical Association, toxic. Instead, Jackson died after suffering for years from an assortment of maladies, including dropsy, heart disease, kidney failure, and chronic tuberculosis. In other words, though the president may have lived a most unnatural life, he died a natural death.[268]

The case of James Buchanan (15th US president, 1857–61), whose status as the only bachelor president has fueled speculation that he may have been "the first gay president in American history." Although

Buchanan in his lifetime was widely rumored to be gay, there is little if any hard, convincing evidence to prove this. This didn't stop his critics from using his supposed homosexuality against him, for personal and political gain. Historian and prolific biographer Jean H. Baker, however, suggests there *is* evidence, at the very least, of Buchanan's *asexuality*, and a factor in her reasoning leading to this conclusion is surprising—the president's hairline. "The best speculation about the sexuality of the nonshaving Buchanan," she asserts, "is that he had little interest in sex," because "in his portraits [he] has eunuch-like, endomorphic features of body and face as well as the low hairline characteristic of asexual men with low levels of testosterone."[269] Unfortunately, Baker provides no further evidence or explanation to elucidate this theory of the hairline.

The case of Grover Cleveland (22nd and 24th US president; 1885–89, 1893–97), the only president to serve two nonconsecutive terms. Just months into his second term of office, in May 1893, the walrus-mustachioed blimp of a man, weighing some three hundred pounds, felt a little bump on the upper left roof of his mouth, back by the molars, on his "cigar-chewing side." He thought nothing of it until the next month, when the bump had blossomed and spread, painfully and unmistakably, into a tumor inching close to his eye. Meeting secretly with his doctors, the diagnosis was rendered quickly: cancer, and it had to be removed. Cancer, back then, with the strong stigma attached to it, was an illness only whispered about. It was deemed "the dread disease" by the press at the time, and so any and all measures were taken to hide the story from the public, which was already angst-ridden due to the ongoing economic depression dubbed the Panic of

1893. But how and where to perform the surgery, away from the prying eyes of the press, became an issue of intense (private) debate. The solution? Tell the public that the president was taking a short fishing vacation, sailing upon a friend's yacht. And sail the president did, vanishing for five days, but not for fishing: the secret surgery occurred instead, aboard the moving boat. The danger of the at-sea operation—conducted by six surgeons who removed the tumor through the president's mouth, along with five teeth and a portion of his jaw—is impossible to overestimate, as author Matthew Algeo has detailed.

As he explained to NPR: "The doctors took incredible risks. . . . They did it very quickly—a similar operation today would take several hours. They did it in 90 minutes. So, it was really an extraordinary achievement in American medicine, but it was a complete secret."[270] And the key to keeping the public in the dark about the operation (in addition to disparaging a reporter who was onto the true story) was the president's famed facial hair—by no means could the surgeons remove the president's trademark mustache. Hair was critical to the cover-up.

THE FUTURE OF HAIR AND HISTORY

If past is prologue, then hair will remain a rich prism by which to glean insights into historic figures, including the US presidents. In fact, according to current scientific thinking, hair as a forensic tool is well poised to play an even greater role in our lives and understanding of the world. Why? Because of the rich font of information encoded in the proteins of human hair.

Hair as a forensic tool is well poised to play an even greater role in our lives and understanding of the world.

Biochemist Glendon Parker is one of the many researchers involved in this exciting new frontier of research, and they believe they stand on the threshold of a breakthrough in forensic science. DNA, they point out, can degrade in the environment, whereas protein is far more stable and chemically robust and can persist for longer periods, which is why they're so excited about the emerging field of *proteomics*, the large-scale analysis of proteins. As the Parker Lab at the University of California (Davis) explains, "Our laboratory seeks to expand the scope of forensic evidence. Difficult evidence

Hair under chemical analysis in a forensic lab.

types, such as hair shafts, trace evidence, bones, and teeth, often have partial or no DNA present in a sample, but they will have protein. Our project uses proteomic genotyping to systematically and sensitively extract genetic information from these samples and use it to assist in forensic or anthropological investigation."[271]

Interestingly, the difference between protein and DNA analysis has been likened to the difference between *reading* Shakespeare and experiencing Shakespeare *live*. As explained in *Introduction to Forensic Proteomics* (2019), edited by Eric D. Merkley:

> DNA provides the instructions, but it is largely proteins that carry out the instructions. The different information provided by protein and DNA analysis can be likened to a Shakespearean play. If DNA provides the script, proteins are the set, the stage crew, and the actors. Reading *King Lear* can be entertaining, inspiring, and thought-provoking. It will certainly leave you in no doubt as to which play you are reading. But it is not the same experience as seeing a well-executed live production of the play. In a similar way, DNA analysis identifies the organisms in question and reveals their potential, but proteomics measures how that genetic potential is realized under given conditions. . . . [A]pplied to questions of crime and criminal justice—but also in areas that have scientifically related problems, such as national security and biodefense, paleontology, archaeology, and cultural history . . . proteomics can answer questions that DNA analysis cannot.[272]

It is for this reason that Parker and his colleagues have called this new research method a potential "game changer for forensics."[273]

Clearly, few tools for understanding the human animal—past or present, socially or scientifically, culturally or chemically—can match or surpass the vast, surprising, and multidimensional power of our tresses. For hair—as I hope this book has demonstrated—is seldom, if ever, simply *hair*.

NOTES

1. Jackie Calmes, "When a Boy Found a Familiar Feel in a Pat of the Head of State," *The New York Times*, May 23, 2012.
2. Ibid.
3. Grant McCracken, *Big Hair: A Journey into the Transformation of Self* (Toronto: Viking, 1995), 14.
4. Judges 13–16; Matthew 10:26–31; John 12:1–8; John 13:1–17 (NIV).
5. Victoria Sherrow, *Encyclopedia of Hair: A Cultural History* (Westport: Greenwood Press, 2006), xxi–xxv, 140–42.
6. Norbert Haas, Francoise Toppe, and Beate M. Henze, "Hairstyles in the Arts of Greek and Roman Antiquity," *Journal of Investigative Dermatology Symposium Proceedings*, volume 10, no. 3 (December 2005): 298–300; Sherrow, *Encyclopedia of Hair*, 334–35; Getty, "No Pain, No Rogaine: Hair Loss and Hairstyle in Ancient Rome," https://www.getty.edu/news/no-pain-no-rogaine-hair-loss-and-hairstyle-in-ancient-rome/.
7. "Hair of the Prophet," *The New York Times*, January 3, 1964; Ustadh Abdullah Anik Misra, "Preservation of the Prophet's Hair and Seeking Blessings Through It," Seekersguidance.org, The Global Islamic Academy; Sherrow, *Encyclopedia of Hair*, 15.
8. Erin Blakemore, "The Political Power of Marie Antoinette's Hair," JSTOR Daily, September 5, 2016, daily.jstor.org; Will Bashor, *Marie Antoinette's Head: The Royal Hairdresser, the Queen, and the Revolution* (Guilford: Lyons Press, 2013), passim.
9. Tiffany May, "Japanese Student Forced to Dye Her Hair Black Wins, and Loses, in Court," *The New York Times*, February 19, 2021.
10. Richard C. Salter, "Shooting Dreads on Sight," in *Millennialism, Persecution, and*

Violence: Historical Cases, ed. Catherine Wessinger (Syracuse: Syracuse University Press, 2000), 101.

11. Scott Lowe, *Hair* (Bloomsbury, 2016), 105–106; Sherrow, 148–152; Matthew Moore, "Facebook 'Kick a Ginger' campaign prompts attacks on redheads," *The Telegraph*, November 22, 2008.

12. Vanessa Friedman, "Buzzed: The Politics of Hair," *The New York Times*, April 5, 2018.

13. Timothy W. Ryback, "Evidence of Evil," *The New Yorker*, November 7, 1993.

14. Deborah Pergament, "It's Not Just Hair: Historical and Cultural Considerations for an Emerging Technology," *Chicago-Kent Law Review* 75, no. 1 (December 1999): 41–59.

15. Few individuals have been more written about than Abraham Lincoln, and there are scores of biographies for gleaning the basic facts of his life and death. My favorites include David Herbert Donald, *Lincoln* (New York: Simon & Schuster, 1995); Michael Burlingame, *Abraham Lincoln: A Life* (Baltimore: John Hopkins University Press, 2023); Allen C. Guelzo, *Abraham Lincoln: Redeemer President* (Grand Rapids: Eerdmans, 1999); Harold Holzer, *Lincoln at Cooper Union: The Speech That Made Abraham Lincoln President* (New York: Simon & Schuster, 2004); Doris Kearns Goodwin, *Team of Rivals: The Political Genius of Abraham Lincoln* (New York: Simon & Schuster, 2005); William Lee Miller, *President Lincoln: The Duty of a Statesman* (New York: Knopf, 2008); Ronald C. White, *A. Lincoln: A Biography* (New York: Random House, 2009); David Alan Johnson, *The Last Weeks of Abraham Lincoln: A Day-by-Day Account of His Personal, Political, and Military Challenges* (Amherst: Prometheus Books, 2018); and Jon Meacham, *And There Was Light: Abraham Lincoln and the American Struggle* (New York: Random House, 2022).

16. For a riveting fictional but fact-based account of the life and death of Henry and Clara Rathbone, and of their experience with the Lincolns at Ford's Theatre on the night of the assassination, see Thomas Mallon's wonderful *Henry and Clara: A Novel* (New York: Ticknor & Fields, 1994); see also Frederick Hatch, *Protecting President Lincoln: The Security Effort, the Thwarted Plots and the Disaster at Ford's Theatre* (Jefferson: McFarland, 2011), 161; and Suzanne W. Hallstrom and Stephan A. Whitlock, "Major Henry Reed Rathbone mtDNA Study," Genetic Lincoln, geneticlincoln.com.

17. Philip Reilly, *Abraham Lincoln's DNA and Other Adventures in Genetics* (Cold Spring Harbor: Cold Spring Harbor Laboratory Press, 2000), 3–13; Jamie Ducharme, "Abraham Lincoln Was Our Tallest President Ever. This May Be Why," *Time*, February 12, 2018; Glenna R. Schroeder-Lein, *Lincoln and Medicine* (Carbondale: Southern Illinois University Press, 2012), 37–49.

18. "Abraham Lincoln," *Charleston Mercury*, Thursday, June 7, 1860, newspapers.com, https://www.newspapers.com/image/605491168/. The writer is responding to a portrait published in *Harper's Weekly*, Vol. 4, no. 178, (May 26, 1860), archive.org, https://archive.org/details/harpersweeklyv4bonn/page/320/mode/2up?view=theater.

19. "Scenes in the Black Republican Convention. The Nominee." *The Weekly Telegraph* (Houston), vol. 26, no. 12 (Tuesday, June 5, 1860), Portal to Texas History, https://texashistory.unt.edu/ark:/67531/metapth236096/m1/2/.

20. David Von Drehle, *Rise to Greatness: Abraham Lincoln and America's Most Perilous Year* (New York: Henry Holt, 2012), 48.

21. Garry Wills, *Lincoln at Gettysburg: The Words That Remade America* (New York: Simon & Schuster, 1992), passim.

22. Mark Bowden, "'Idiot,' 'Yahoo,' 'Original Gorilla': How Lincoln Was Dissed in His Day," *The Atlantic*, June 2013.

23. Walt Whitman's Letter to Nathaniel Bloom and John F. S. Gray, March 19–20, 1863, reproduced at the whitmanarchive.org.

24. Nathaniel Hawthorne, "Chiefly About War Matters," *The Atlantic Monthly*, July 1862, reproduced at theatlantic.com and https://www.ibiblio.org/eldritch/nh/cawm.html.

25. Harold Holzer interview by Megan Gambino, "Lincoln the Homely," *Civil War Times Illustrated*, February 2008, https://www.smithsonianmag.com/history/ask-an-expert-what-did-abraham-lincolns-voice-sound-like-13446201/.

26. Interview with Lincoln scholar Harold Holzer, "What Did Abraham Lincoln's Voice Sound Like?" *Smithsonian Magazine* online, June 6, 2011.

27. Richard Wightman Fox, *Lincoln's Body: A Cultural History* (New York: W. W. Norton, 2015), 8.

28. Jacques Barzun, "Lincoln's Philosophic Vision," (21st Fortenbaugh Lecture, Gettysburg College, Gettysburg, PA, 1982); see also, Donald T. Phillips, *Lincoln on Leadership* (New York: Warner Books, 1992).

29. Tony Kushner, *Lincoln*, International Movie Script Database, https://imsdb.com/scripts/Lincoln.html.

30. "The Advice of a Little Girl," Library of Congress Exhibition, March 2009, https://www.loc.gov/loc/lcib/0903/letter.html; Abraham Lincoln papers: Series 1. General Correspondence. 1833–1916: Abraham Lincoln to Grace Bedell, Friday, October 19, 1860, Library of Congress; Donald, *Lincoln*, 258.

31. Burlingame, *Lincoln: A Life*, Volume Two, 18; Sara Kettler, "The Surprising Reason Abraham Lincoln Grew a Beard," biography.com, February 11, 2020, https://www.biography.com/political-figures/abraham-lincoln-beard.

32. James J. Shea, "The Milton Bradley Story" (Lecture: New York: Newcomen Society in North America, 1973), 10; Kettler, "The Surprising Reason."

33. "The Passing of the Beard," *Harper's Weekly* 47 (1903): 102; "The Forgotten Plague: TB's Surprising Results," *The American Experience*, pbs.org.

34. Tim Jones, "Dewey defeats Truman: The most famous wrong call in electoral history," *Chicago Tribune*, October 31, 2020; Ben Cosgrove, "Behind the Picture: 'Dewey Defeats Truman' and the Politics of Memory," *Time*, May 4, 2014.

35. Christoper Oldstone-Moore, *Of Beards and Men: The Revealing History of Facial Hair* (Chicago: University of Chicago Press, 2016), 232.

36. Lance Morrow, "Al Gore, and Other Famous Bearded Men," *Time*, August 16, 2001.

37. "Woman Urging Lincoln's Beard Passes in West," *Schenectady Gazette*, November 4, 1936.

38. Daniel Stashower, "The Unsuccessful Plot to Kill Abraham Lincoln," *Smithsonian Magazine,* February 2013.

39. Ibid.

40. Diplomatic missive from US Secretary of State William Seward, Department of State, Washington, DC, July 15, 1862.

41. Paul Martin, "Lincoln's Missing Bodyguard," *Smithsonian Magazine* online, April 7, 2010, https://www.smithsonianmag.com/history/lincolns-missing-bodyguard-12932069/.

42. Quoted in Francis B. Carpenter, *Six Months at the White House: The Story of a Picture* (New York: Hurd and Houghton, 1866), 281.

43. Goodwin, *Team of Rivals*, 734–5.

44. Brad Meltzer and Josh Mensch, *The Lincoln Conspiracy: The Secret Plot to Kill America's 16th President—and Why It Failed* (New York: Flatiron Books, 2020), 150.

45. Holzer, "Lincoln the Homely," *Civil War Times*, February 2008.

46. Harold Holzer, "Like a Thief in the Night," *The New York Times*, February 22, 2011; Alexander K. McClure, *Abraham Lincoln and Men of War-Times* (Philadelphia: Times Publishing Co., 1892), 45.

47. Dr. Leale gave varying accounts of his actions on the night of the assassination. See Charles A. Leale's "Lincoln's Last Hours," a speech delivered in New York in 1909 on the hundredth anniversary of Lincoln's birth; Helena Iles Papaioannou and Daniel W. Stowell, "Dr. Charles A. Leale's Report on the Assassination of Abraham Lincoln," *Journal of the Abraham Lincoln Association* vol. 34, no. 1 (Winter 2013): 40–53; and, for a more general overview of events, Dorothy Meserve Kunhardt, Philip B. Kunhardt Jr., and Bruce Catton, *Twenty Days: A Narrative in Text and Pictures of the Assassination of Abraham Lincoln and the Twenty Days and Nights that Followed—the Nation in Mourning, the Long Trip Home to Springfield* (New York: Harper & Row, 1965).

48. Fox, *Lincoln's Body*, 34.

49. Harold Holzer and Frank J. Williams, *Lincoln's Deathbed in Art and Memory: The "Rubber Room" Phenomenon* (Gettysburg: Thomas Publications, 1998).

50. E. Lawrence Abel, *A Finger in Lincoln's Brain: What Modern Science Reveals About Lincoln, His Assassination, and Its Aftermath* (Santa Barbara: Praeger, 2015), 80–83.

51. Candice Millard, *Destiny of the Republic: A Tale of Madness, Medicine, and the Murder of a President* (New York: Doubleday, 2011); Howard Markel, "The Dirty, Painful Death of President James A. Garfield," pbs.org, September 16, 2016, https://www.pbs.org/newshour/health/dirty-painful-death-president-james-garfield.

52. "Abraham Lincoln's Final Hours, Death, and Autopsy Report Documented by Dr. Robert Stone," Shapell Manuscript Foundation, shapell.org, April 15, 1865, https://www.shapell.org/manuscript/doctor-of-abraham-lincoln-obervation-of-presidents-last-hours-alive-and-postmortem/; "The Autopsy of President Abraham Lincoln," National Library of Medicine, nlm.nih.gov.
53. Fox, *Lincoln's Body*, 43.
54. Adam Gopnik, "Angels and Ages—Abraham Lincoln's Words, Maybe," *The New Yorker,* May 21, 2007.
55. "Upstairs at the White House: Prince of Wales Room," The Lehrman Institute, mrlincolnswhitehouse.org.
56. "Treasures of the White House: The Lincoln Bed," The White House Historical Association, whitehousehistory.org.
57. Goodwin, *Team of Rivals*, 332.
58. "The Lincoln Funeral Train," University of Illinois, Illinois History & Lincoln Collections, publish.illinois.edu, August 30, 2019.
59. Gary Laderman, *The Sacred Remains: American Attitudes Toward Death, 1799–1883* (New Haven: Yale University Press, 1996), passim.
60. Richard Bak, *The Day Lincoln Was Shot* (Dallas: Taylor, 1998), 138.
61. Bak, *The Day*, 139.
62. Jill L. Newmark and Roxanne Beatty, "The Lincoln Autopsy," *Circulating Now: From the Historical Collections of the National Library of Medicine*, National Library of Medicine, April 16, 2015, https://circulatingnow.nlm.nih.gov/2015/04/16/the-lincoln-autopsy/#:~:text=Seated%20around%20the%20room%20were,soul%20of%20a%20great%20nation.%E2%80%9D.
63. Ibid.
64. Fox, *Lincoln's Body*, 66.
65. William Henry Herndon and Jesse William Weik, *Herndon's Lincoln: The True Story of a Great Life . . . The History and Personal Recollections of Abraham Lincoln* (Springfield: The Herndon's Lincoln Publishing Company, 1921), 375, https://archive.org/details/herndonslincolnt02herndon.
66. Fox, *Lincoln's Body*, 9.
67. Ibid., prefatory quote.
68. W. E. B. Du Bois, "Again, Lincoln," *The Crisis*, September 1922, 200.
69. Michael Beschloss, "When T. R. Saw Lincoln," *The New York Times*, May 21, 2014.
70. Letter from John Hay to Theodore Roosevelt, July 27, 1898. The full quote reads, "It has been a splendid little war, begun with the highest motives, carried on with magnificent intelligence and spirit, favored by that Fortune which loves the brave."
71. Jessica Contrera, "Why did someone just pay $35,000 for John Lennon's hair?" *The Washington Post*, February 21, 2016.

72. Nicole Bode and Xana O'Neill, "Authentic Britney hair on sale for $1 million," *The Seattle Times*, February 19, 2007.

73. "LifeGem to make diamonds out of Jackson's hair," *Economic Times*, July 30, 2009; see also LifeGem's website at lifegem.com.

74. Jerry Guo, "A Little Off the Top for History," *The New York Times*, July 13, 2008.

75. Rick Rojas, "Finding a Lock of George Washington's Hair, and a Link to American History," *The New York Times*, February 18, 2018.

76. Ibid.

77. "Hair Ornaments," *Godey's Lady's Book*, Volume 61, 1860, 181.

78. Gerrick D. Kennedy, "Michael Jackson's hair auctioned off for $10,871," *Los Angeles Times*, December 12, 2011; RR Auction, Lot 85, "John Dillinger Hair and Melvin Purvis Signed Memorandum Display," September 29, 2012.

79. Tony Perrottet, "Gentlemen, Charge Your Indecent Props!" *Slate,* December 18, 2009.

80. Olivia B. Waxman, "These Strands of Lincoln's Locks Could Sell for Thousands of Dollars. What's Behind the Fascination With Presidential Hair?" *Time*, August 23, 2018.

81. "A Room with a View on History: The Petersen House," Ford's Theatre Blog, March 18, 2015.

82. James L. Swanson, "The Blood Relics From the Lincoln Assassination," *Smithsonian Magazine,* March 2015.

83. Heritage Auctions, "Abraham Lincoln: Superbly Documented Lock of Hair," January 24, 2015; Associated Press, "Lock of Lincoln's hair part of $800K lot auctioned in Dallas," *The State Journal-Register*, January 24, 2015.

84. Swanson, "Blood Relics."

85. Fox, *Lincoln's Body*, 352; Robert Reyburn, *Fifty Years in the Practice of Medicine and Surgery, 1856–1906* (Washington, DC: Beresford, 1907), 20; Jon Haworth, "Lock of Hair Taken From Abraham Lincoln During Postmortem Exam Sold at Auction," abcnews.go.com, September 14, 2020.

86. "Abraham Lincoln: Approximately Twenty-Five Strands of Hair Formerly Owned by Alexander Gardner," Heritage Auctions, August 25, 2018; Tim Teeman, "Buy Lincoln's Hair—and His Assassin's," *Daily Beast*, July 12, 2017; Abel, *A Finger in Lincoln's Brain*, 183–84.

87. John Taliaferro, *All the Great Prizes: The Life of John Hay, from Lincoln to Roosevelt* (New York, Simon & Schuster, 2013), 171.

88. Taliaferro, *All the Great Prizes*, 311.

89. Ibid., 531.

90. David C. Mearns, "Exquisite Collector, or the Scalping of Abraham Lincoln," *Journal of the Illinois State Historical Society*, vol. 52, no. 1, (spring 1959): 45–51.

91. Theodore Roosevelt, *An Autobiography* (New York: The Macmillan Company, 1913), 420.

92. Robert McCracken Peck, "George Washington's Brush with Immortality: The Hair Relics of a Sainted Hero," *The Magazine Antiques*, July 30, 2015; Rick Rojas, "Finding a Lock of George Washington's Hair, and a Link to American History," *The New York Times*, February 18, 2018; "Lock of George Washington's hair sold for nearly $40K," CNN, April 6, 2021; Danielle Cinone, "Lock of George Washington's hair sells for $35G in auction," *New York Daily News*, February 4, 2019.

93. Letter from George Washington to Catharine Wilhelmina Livingston, March 18, 1778, Founders Online, National Archives online, https://founders.archives.gov /documents/Washington/03-14-02-0188.

94. Margaret C. Conkling, *Memoirs of the Mother and Wife of Washington* (New York and Auburn: Miller, Orton, and Mulligan, 1855), 214–215.

95. Peck, "George Washington's Brush with Immortality," *The Magazine Antiques*.

96. Ibid.

97. Ibid.

98. "John Varden's Washington Museum," *Souvenir Nation,* National Museum of American History, americanhistory.si.edu; Courtney Fullilove, "The hair of distinguished persons in the patent office building museum," *Museum History Journal*, 2017.

99. Robert McCracken Peck*, Specimens of Hair: The Curious Collection of Peter A. Browne* (New York: Blast Books, 2018), passim; Peck, "Hair: The Pile Albums of Peter A. Browne," *Natural History*, December 2018/January 2019.

100. Clifton Crais and Pamela Scully, *Sara Baartman and the Hottentot Venus: A Ghost Story and a Biography* (Princeton: Princeton University Press, 2009).

101. "Message from the Peabody Director," Peabody Museum of Archaeology and Ethnology, November 10, 2022, https://peabody.harvard.edu/news/message-peabody-director.

102. Tarah D. Giles, "Harvard Pledges to Return Hundreds of Native American Hair Samples Housed at Peabody Museum," *The Harvard Crimson*, November 12, 2022, https://www.thecrimson.com/article/2022/11/12/peabody-hair-samples/.

103. Becky Little, "Long Before Trump, We Were Obsessed With Presidential Hair*," National Geographic*, February 18, 2018.

104. Robert McCracken Peck in discussion with the author, July 29, 2022.

105. "President Ronald Reagan's Hair," Heritage Auctions, February 21, 2006; "Gerald Ford: Three Silver Brushes," Heritage Auctions, December 11, 2012.

106. "Collection of Ulysses S. Grant's Strands of Hair Encased in a Gold Locket," Nate D. Sanders Auctions, July 31, 2014; "Someone bought a lock of Thomas Jefferson's hair for nearly $7,000," Associated Press, May 16, 2016; William L. Bird Jr., *Souvenir Nation: Relics, Keepsakes, and Curios from the Smithsonian's National Museum of American History* (New York: Princeton Architectural Press, 2013), 128.

107. "Lee Harvey Oswald's toe tag hammers for $56,000," Paul Fraser Collectibles, November 9, 2017.

108. "First Murder on Television," Guinness World Records, n.d., guinnessworldrecords .com/world-records/first-murder-on-television.

109. James L. Swanson, *End of Days: The Assassination of John F. Kennedy* (New York: William Morrow, 2013), 178.

110. Clint Hill and Lisa McCubbin, *Five Days in November* (New York: Gallery Books, 2013), 139.

111. Ibid., 158.

112. Ibid., 160.

113. Peter Collier and David Horowitz, *The Kennedys: An American Drama* (New York: Summit Books, 1984), 314; Hill, *Five Days*, 160.

114. Nina Totenberg, "Justice Ruth Bader Ginsburg, Champion of Gender Equality, Dies at 87," *Weekend Edition*, NPR, September 18, 2020.

115. Courtney Weaver, "Nancy Pelosi entangled in US hair salon scandal," *Financial Times*, September 4, 2020.

116. Thomas L. Friedman, "Haircut Grounded Clinton While the Price Took Off," *The New York Times*, May 21, 1993.

117. Angelique Chrisafis, "Bad hair days for François Hollande over €10,000 coiffeur bill," *The Guardian*, July 13, 2016.

118. Brooke Singman, "Pelosi Used Shuttered San Francisco Hair Salon for Blow-Out, Owner Calls It 'Slap in the Face'," Fox News, September 1, 2020, https://www .foxnews.com/politics/pelosi-san-francisco-hair-salon-owner-calls-it-slap-in-the-face.

119. Jeffrey Goldberg, "Trump: Americans Who Died in War Are 'Losers' and 'Suckers,'" *The Atlantic*, September 3, 2020, https://www.theatlantic.com/politics/archive /2020/09/trump-americans-who-died-at-war-are-losers-and-suckers/615997/.

120. Joe Mellor, "Trump comes under heavy criticism for missing Armistice Day memorial due to heavy rain," *The London Economic*, November 11, 2018.

121. Goldberg, "Trump."

122. Eun Kyung Kim, "Donald Trump lets Jimmy Fallon wreck his hair on *Tonight Show*," today.com, September 16, 2016.

123. Gaius Suetonius Tranquillus, *Divus Julius*, Suet. Jul. 45, perseus.tufts.edu; Andrea Frediani, "Julius Caesar Came. He Saw. He Conquered. Here's How Rome Celebrated," *National Geographic*, July 10, 2019.

124. Dan Fitzpatrick, "The Dark History Behind Donald Trump's Hair," The National Memo, June 12, 2016.

125. Emily Jacobs, "*The Atlantic*'s Jeffrey Goldberg Says Anonymous Sources Are 'Not Good Enough,'" *New York Post*, September 9, 2020.

126. Kayleigh McEnany, *For Such a Time as This: My Faith Journey through the White House and Beyond* (New York: Post Hill Press, 2021), 105.

127. Jack Holmes, "Joe Biden Talking About Kids Touching His Hairy Legs in a Swimming Pool Is Not Great Viewing," *Esquire,* December 2, 2019.

128. "Yale University Class Day Address," C-SPAN, May 20, 2001.

129. Alyson Walsh, "The Hillary Clinton Look: Power Hair, Pantsuits and Practicality," *The Guardian*, April 15, 2015.

130. "YouGov Survey: Civics Test," yougov, June 14–17, 2022, https://today.yougov.com/politics/articles/42981-us-civics-test-yougov-poll-june-14–17–2022.

131. Taylor Orth, "Can Americans pass a civics test for US naturalization?" yougov.com, June 28, 2022, https://today.yougov.com/politics/articles/42984-can-americans-pass-civics-test-us-naturalization?redirect_from=%2Ftopics%2Fpolitics%2Farticles-reports%2F2022%2F06%2F28%2Fcan-americans-pass-civics-test-us-naturalization.

132. Walter Isaacson, *Benjamin Franklin: An American Life* (New York: Simon & Schuster, 2003), Chapters 13–15, passim.

133. Thomas Fleming, "Franklin Charms Paris," *American Heritage*, Spring 2010.

134. Ibid.

135. Letter from Benjamin Franklin to Sarah Bache, June 3, 1779; reproduced at Founders Online, National Archives online, https://founders.archives.gov/documents/Franklin/01-29-02-0496.

136. Joanna M. Gohmann, "Ambassador in a Hat: The Sartorial Power of Benjamin Franklin's Fur Cap," *The Junto,* February 15, 2017.

137. Paul Elmer More, *Benjamin Franklin* (Boston: Houghton Mifflin, 1900; Project Gutenberg, 2009), https://www.gutenberg.org/files/29482/29482-h/29482-h.htm.

138. Martin Dugard and Bill O'Reilly, *Killing England: The Brutal Struggle for American Independence* (New York: Henry Holt, 2017), 155–57.

139. From Benjamin Franklin to Emma Thompson, February 8, 1777, reproduced at Founders Online, National Archives online, https://founders.archives.gov/documents/Franklin/01-23-02-0188#BNFN-01-23-02-0188-fn-0002.

140. Leo Janos, "The Last Days of the President," *The Atlantic Monthly*, July 1973, https://www.theatlantic.com/magazine/archive/1973/07/the-last-days-of-the-president/376281/; Kevin Townsend, "LBJ's Wild Ex-President Hair (And the Story Behind It)," *The Atlantic*, August 24, 2018.

141. "The Accidental President," Truman Library Institute online, October 18, 2017.

142. "Longhand Note of Judge Harry S. Truman," May 1931, Harry S. Truman Papers, Harry S. Truman Library and Museum.

143. David McCullough, *Truman* (New York: Simon & Schuster, 1992), story recalled by author in interview with C-SPAN, June 27, 2020.

144. Tammy Williams, "'I Never Wanted to Do Anything as Badly in My Life': Bess Truman Bobs Her Hair," National Archives online, Pieces of History, June 12, 2020,

https://prologue.blogs.archives.gov/2020/06/12/i-never-wanted-to-do-anything-as
-badly-in-my-life-bess-truman-bobs-her-hair/.

145. Gilbert King, "General Grant in Love and War," *Smithsonian Magazine*, smithsonianmag
.com, February 14, 2012.

146. Ibid.

147. Lillian Cunningham, "The Doting, Devoted Love Letters of Ulysses S. Grant," *The Washington Post*, May 8, 2016; *My Dearest Julia: The Wartime Letters of Ulysses S. Grant to His Wife* (New York: Library of America, 2018).

148. Robert C. Belding, "Ulysses S. Grant: Chronic Malaria and the myth of his alcoholism," *Journal of Medical Biography*, March 8, 2022.

149. Ronald C. White, *American Ulysses: A Life of Ulysses S. Grant* (New York: Random House, 2016), 317–18; Charles Bracelen Flood, *Grant and Sherman: The Friendship that Won the Civil War* (New York: Farrar, Straus and Giroux, 2005), 227–28.

150. "Collection of Ulysses S. Grant's Strands of Hair Encased in a Gold Locket," Nate D. Sanders Auctions, July 31, 2014.

151. David Greenberg, "Calvin Coolidge: Life Before the Presidency," The Miller Center, University of Virginia, millercenter.org.

152. Ibid.; Amity Shlaes, *Coolidge* (New York: Harper, 2014), 4.

153. "Grace Coolidge Overview," Calvin Coolidge Presidential Foundation, coolidgefoundation.org.

154. Shlaes, *Coolidge*, 298–99.

155. Lawrence L. Knutson, "The Death of a Son: Calvin Coolidge Jr.," in "Death and the White House," *Quarterly Journal of the White House Historical Association* (Fall 2017): 54–59; Joshua Kendall, *First Dads: Parenting and Politics from George Washington to Barack Obama* (New York: Grand Central Publishing, 2016), 274–75.

156. Shlaes, *Coolidge*, 24, 300; Kendall, *First Dads*, 274–75.

157. Quoted by Mark Bushnell, in "History: The Pain Behind Calvin Coolidge's Silence," *Rutland Herald*, October 17, 2018; Benjamin Shapell, "Calvin Coolidge Jr.'s Death," The Shapell Manuscript Foundation online, July 6, 2017.

158. Robert Dallek, "The Medical Ordeals of JFK," *The Atlantic Monthly*, December 2002; Kendall, *First Dads*, 276–77; see also, Robert E. Gilbert, *The Tormented President: Calvin Coolidge, Death, and Clinical Depression* (Westport, Connecticut: Praeger Publishers, 2003).

159. Calvin Coolidge, *The Autobiography of Calvin Coolidge* (New York: Cosmopolitan Book Company, 1929), 190.

160. Steven Watts, *JFK and the Masculine Mystique: Sex and Power on the New Frontier* (New York: Thomas Dunne Books, 2016), 158; Mark White, "Apparent Perfection: The Image of John F. Kennedy," *History*, 2013: 236.

161. John Pearson, *The Life of Ian Fleming* (New York: McGraw-Hill, 1966), 300–01; "Ian Fleming and JFK . . . 50 Years Later," Literary007.com, November 28, 2013.

162. Andrew Lycett, *Ian Fleming* (London: Weidenfeld & Nicolson, 1995), 367–68.

163. *Alleged Assassination Plots Involving Foreign Leaders: An Interim Report of the Select Committee to Study Governmental Operations*, US Senate, November 20, 1975, 72.

164. Stephen Kinzer, *The Brothers: John Foster Dulles, Allen Dulles, and Their Secret World War: John Foster Dulles, Allen Dulles, and Their Secret World War* (2013), 274.

165. Dallek, "The Medical Ordeals of JFK," *The Atlantic Monthly*, December 2002; James N. Giglio, *The Presidency of John F. Kennedy* (Lawrence: University Press of Kansas, 1991), 263–64; Peter Keating, "The Strange Saga of JFK and the Original 'Dr. Feelgood,'" *New York Magazine*, November 22, 2013; Martin Kasindorf's 2013 documentary, *Everybody Went to Max: Remembering Dr. Feelgood, the Merlin of Kennedy's Camelot*.

166. Barbara A. Perry and Alfred Reaves IV, "Inside the Unsung Life of the Man Who Was John F. Kennedy's Most Personal Assistant," *Time*, November 20, 2018.

167. "Scholarly Analysis of the Kennedy-Nixon Debates," Purdue University Department of History online, https://www.cla.purdue.edu/academic/history/debate/kennedynixon /kennedynixonscholarly.html.

168. Quoted by Dan Gunderman in "The story of the first TV presidential debate between Nixon and Kennedy—'My God, they've embalmed him before he even died,'" *New York Daily News,* September 24, 2016.

169. David Greenberg, "Rewinding the Kennedy-Nixon Debates: Did JFK really win because he looked better on television?" *Slate*, September 24, 2010.

170. "Scholarly Analysis of the Kennedy-Nixon Debates," Purdue University Department of History online; Paul Myron Hillier, "Rethinking Media and Technology: What the Kennedy-Nixon Debate Myth Can Really Teach Us," *Online Journal of Communication and Media Technologies*, vol. 5, no. 2 (April 2015).

171. Greenberg, "Rewinding the Kennedy-Nixon Debates."

172. Martin Dugard and Bill O'Reilly, *Killing Kennedy: The End of Camelot* (New York: Henry Holt, 2016), 258, 268.

173. Larry J. Sabato, *The Kennedy Half Century: The Presidency, Assassination, and Lasting Legacy of John F. Kennedy* (New York: Bloomsbury, 2013), 424.

174. Sarah Bradford, *America's Queen: The Life of Jacqueline Kennedy Onassis* (New York: Viking, 2000), 95.

175. Caitlin Flanagan, "Jackie and the Girls: Mrs. Kennedy's JFK Problem—and Ours," *The Atlantic*, July/August 2012.

176. Mimi Alford, *Once Upon a Secret: My Affair with President John F. Kennedy and Its Aftermath* (New York: Random House, 2012), 48–56.

177. Ibid., 77.

178. Ibid., 82.

179. Ibid., 104.

180. Ibid., 100–101.

181. Ibid., 127.

182. Michael F. Holt, *Franklin Pierce: The American Presidents Series: The 14th President, 1853–1857* (New York: Times Books, 2010), 1.

183. Ibid., 10–11.

184. Ibid., 28–29.

185. "The Accident at Andover—Death of the Only Son of General Pierce," *Illustrated News*, January 22, 1853.

186. Peter A. Wallner, *Franklin Pierce: New Hampshire's Favorite Son* (Concord: Plaidswede Publishing, 2004), 241–42.

187. *The New York Times*, January 7, 1853; see also Kendall, *First Dads*, 240–47.

188. "Jane Means Appleton Pierce," White House biographies of the First Families, whitehouse.gov; see also, for a concise biography of Jane and her many struggles, "The President's Wife, Jane Means Appleton Pierce: A Woman of Her Time," in "Revealing Relationships: The Family and Friends of Franklin Pierce," *Historical New Hampshire* 59, no. 1 (Spring 2005), 45–63.

189. Description by Abby Means, Jane Pierce's girlhood friend, quoted in Wallner, *Franklin Pierce*, 242.

190. Wallner, *Franklin Pierce*, 251.

191. Ibid., 242.

192. Thomas J. Balcerski, *Bosom Friends: The Intimate World of James Buchanan and William Rufus King* (Oxford: Oxford University Press, 2019).

193. Wallner, *Franklin Pierce*, xi; "Franklin Pierce's Unruly Hair Pondered on Presidents' Day," Associated Press, February 17, 2008.

194. Clayton M. McCleskey, "Waxing the presidency at Madame Tussauds," *The Dallas Morning News*, February 18, 2011.

195. "Franklin Pierce's Unruly Hair," Associated Press.

196. Quoted in "Barbara Bush, former First Lady–obituary," *The Telegraph*, April 18, 2018. Barbara Bush had died the day before.

197. Pamela Kilian, *Barbara Bush: Matriarch of a Dynasty* (New York: Thomas Dunne Books, 2002), 41.

198. Barbara Bush, *Barbara Bush: A Memoir* (New York: Guideposts, 1994), 44.

199. Quoted in George W. Bush, *41: A Portrait of My Father* (New York: Crown Publishers, 2014), 55.

200. Barbara Bush, *A Memoir*, 44.

201. Ibid., 48.

202. Ibid., 49.

203. Jon Meacham, *Destiny and Power: The American Odyssey of George Herbert Walker Bush* (New York: Random House, 2015), 104.

204. George W. Bush, *41*, 52–58, 209.

205. Ibid.

206. Susan Page, *The Matriarch: Barbara Bush and the Making of an American Dynasty* (New York: Twelve Books, 2019), 25.

207. Barbara Bush, *A Memoir*, 46.

208. Doug Wead, *All the President's Children: Triumph and Tragedy in the Lives of America's First Families* (New York: Atria, 2004), 78.

209. George Lardner Jr. and Lois Romano, "Tragedy Created Bush Mother-Son Bond," *The Washington Post*, Monday, July 26, 1999, page A1, https://www.washingtonpost.com/wp-srv/politics/campaigns/wh2000/stories/bush072699.htm.

210. Ibid.

211. Page, *The Matriarch*, 26.

212. "Barbara Pierce Bush," White House biographies of the First Families, whitehouse.gov, https://www.whitehouse.gov/about-the-white-house/first-families/barbara-pierce-bush/.

213. Page, *The Matriarch*, 98–99.

214. Ibid.

215. Ibid., 110.

216. Ibid.

217. "Wellesley Remembers Barbara Bush's Words to the Class of 1990," Wellesley College, wellesley.edu, April 19, 2018.

218. Page, *The Matriarch*, 210–11.

219. Katie Spalding, "'Marie Antoinette Syndrome': The Mysterious Condition That Turns Hair White Overnight," IFLScience, iflscience.com, June 14, 2021.

220. George W. Bush, *41*, 56.

221. "Can Fright Turn Hair Suddenly White?" Live Science, livescience.com, September 26, 2012.

222. Matt Stevens, "Will Smith Hits Chris Rock After Joke About His Wife, Jada," *The New York Times*, March 27, 2022; Jen Juneau, "Chris Rock's Black Hair Doc Explored 'Self-Esteem of the Black Community' Ahead of Oscars Controversy," *People*, March 28, 2022; quotes by Mooney and Long found in the documentary.

223. "Can hair really turn white from fright?" NBC News, nbcnews.com, October 26, 2009.

224. Alexander A. Navarini, Stephan Nobbe, and Ralph M. Trueb, "Marie Antoinette Syndrome," *Archives of Dermatology*, June 2009.

225. Spalding, "'Marie Antoinette Syndrome.'"

226. Ibid.

227. James Breig, "Hair's Breadth: Locks Could Be Keys to Jefferson Mystery," *Colonial Williamsburg Journal*, Autumn 2010.

228. "A Chronology: Key Moments in the Clinton-Lewinsky Saga," CNN.com; David Maraniss, "First Lady Launches Counterattack," *The Washington Post*, January 28, 1998.

229. Kenneth Starr's report to the House of Representatives, reproduced in "Clinton Accused," *The Washington Post*, washingtonpost.com; see also "William J. Clinton: Federal Impeachment," Research Guides, Library of Congress, guides.loc.gov.

230. Joseph J. Ellis, "Jefferson: Post-DNA," *William and Mary Quarterly*, vol. 57, no. 1 (January 2000): 125–38.

231. James Thomson Callender, "The President, Again," September 1, 1802, *The Recorder, or, Lady's and Gentleman's Miscellany*, a Federalist newspaper in Richmond, Virginia, reproduced in the *Encyclopedia Virginia*, encyclopediavirginia.org.

232. Joseph J. Ellis, "'Tom and Sally': The Jefferson-Hemings Paternity Debate," *Encyclopaedia Britannica*, britannica.com, May 14, 2012, https://www.britannica.com /topic/Tom-and-Sally-the-Jefferson-Hemings-paternity-debate-1688375.

233. Madison Hemings, "Life Among the Lowly, No. 1," *Pike County Republican*, Waverly, Ohio, March 13, 1873; reproduced in *Encyclopedia Virginia*, encyclopediavirginia.org.

234. "Sally Hemings," monticello.org.

235. Henry S. Randall, *The Life of Thomas Jefferson* (New York: Derby & Jackson, 1858), 1:34, 63.

236. Randall, *The Life of Thomas Jefferson*, 1:382.

237. Fawn M. Brodie, *Thomas Jefferson: An Intimate History* (New York: W. W. Norton, 2010), 209.

238. Dugard and O'Reilly, *Killing England*, 301.

239. Randall, *The Life of Thomas Jefferson*, 1:384; Andrew Burstein and Catherine Mowbray, "Jefferson and Sterne," *Early American Literature*, vol. 29, no. 1 (1994): 20.

240. Charles B. Van Pelt, "Thomas Jefferson and Maria Cosway," *American Heritage*, August 1971.

241. "Thomas Jefferson's Head, Heart, and Wrist," *Plodding Through the Presidents*, ploddingthroughthepresidents.com, November 2, 2014; Jon Meacham confirms this description in *Thomas Jefferson: The Art of Power* (New York: Random House, 2012), 197–200.

242. Nan Britton, *The President's Daughter* (New York: Elizabeth Ann Guild, 1927), i, 85.

243. Jordyn Phelps, "Ex-President Warren Harding's Love Child Confirmed Through DNA Testing: Nan Britton Has Been Called the Monica Lewinsky of Her Time," ABC News, August 13, 2015.

244. Peter Baker, "DNA Is Said to Solve a Mystery of Warren Harding's Love Life," *The New York Times*, August 12, 2015.

245. Phelps, "Ex-President Warren Harding's Love Child Confirmed"; Baker, "DNA Is Said to Solve a Mystery of Warren Harding's Love Life."

246. Peter Baker, "DNA Shows Warren Harding Wasn't America's First Black President," *The New York Times*, August 18, 2015.

247. Aditya Agrawal, "DNA Tests Show This President Did Not Have Black Ancestors," *Time*, August 18, 2015; Baker, "DNA Shows."

248. John S. D. Eisenhower, *Zachary Taylor: The American Presidents Series: The 12th President, 1849–1850* (New York: Times Books, 2008), passim.

249. Michael Holt, "Zachary Taylor: Impact and Legacy," The Miller Center, University of Virginia, millercenter.org.

250. Eisenhower, *Zachary Taylor*, 132–34.

251. Benjamin Thompson, *A Funeral Oration on the Death of Zachary Taylor (Late President of the United States), Delivered by Request of the City Council, Charlestown, July 31st, 1850* (Charlestown: Caleb Brand, 1850), 9.

252. Allan B. Schwartz, "Medical Mystery: Did This President Suffer a Death by Cherries?" *The Philadelphia Inquirer*, May 6, 2018.

253. Interview with Clara Rising, C-SPAN Presidential Series, "Life Portrait of Zachary Taylor," May 31, 1999; transcript available at c-span.org.

254. Joan Acocella, "Murder by Poison: The Rise and Fall of Arsenic," *The New Yorker*, October 7, 2013.

255. James C. Whorton, *The Arsenic Century: How Victorian Britain Was Poisoned at Home, Work, and Play* (Oxford: Oxford University Press, 2010), 9.

256. Zachary Crockett, "How Did President Zachary Taylor Actually Die?" Priceonomics, priceonomics.com, July 2, 2015, https://priceonomics.com/how-did-president-zachary-taylor-actually-die/.

257. Ibid.; "Zachary Taylor's Deadly Snack," *Oak Ridge National Laboratory Review*, Oak Ridge National Labroatory, ornl.gov, November 27, 2018, https://www.ornl.gov/blog/ornl-review/zachary-taylor-s-deadly-snack.

258. Ibid.; see also Michel Marriott, "Verdict In: 12th President Was Not Assassinated," *The New York Times*, June 27, 1991.

259. "Turned Over in His Grave," *The New York Times*, June 20, 1991.

260. Andrew Roberts, *The Last King of America: The Misunderstood Reign of George III* (New York: Viking, 2021), 523.

261. Ibid., 3.

262. Roberts, "The Misdiagnosis of 'The King's Malady' as Porphyria," Appendix to *The Last King of America*.

263. "Porphyria," Mayo Clinic, mayoclinic.org, https://www.mayoclinic.org/diseases-conditions/porphyria/symptoms-causes/syc-20356066.

264. "King George III: Mad or misunderstood?" BBC News, July 13, 2004; Michael Schirber, "Doctors Poisoned Crazy King George, Study Finds," Live Science,

livescience.com, July 21, 2005, https://www.livescience.com/328-doctors-poisoned-crazy-king-george-study-finds.html.

265. Ibid.

266. Martin Warren in discussion with the author, May 28, 2022.

267. "King George III: Mad or misunderstood?" BBC News, July 13, 2004; Reuters, "Medication triggered madness of King George," NBC News, July 21, 2005, https://www.nbcnews.com/id/wbna8658128.

268. "Hair samples indicate Andrew Jackson died of kidney failure," *Deseret News*, August 11, 1999.

269. Jean H. Baker, *James Buchanan: The American Presidents Series: The 15th President, 1857–1861* (New York: Times Books, 2004), 26.

270. "A Yacht, a Mustache: How a President Hid His Tumor," *Morning Edition*, NPR, npr.org, July 6, 2011; interview with Matthew Algeo, author of *The President Is a Sick Man: Wherein the Supposedly Virtuous Grover Cleveland Survives a Secret Surgery at Sea and Vilifies the Courageous Newspaperman Who Dared Expose the Truth* (Chicago: Chicago Review Press, 2011), https://www.npr.org/2011/07/06/137621988/a-yacht-a-mustache-how-a-president-hid-his-tumor.

271. "Mission," Parker Lab, parkerlab.ucdavis.edu/mission; see also Marcus Cannon, "Why Hair Analysis Could Become an Alternative to DNA Testing," InterFocus, mynewlab.com, December 14, 2016.

272. Eric D. Merkley, *Introduction to Forensic Proteomics* (Washington, DC.: American Chemical Society, 2019) , https://pubs.acs.org/doi/full/10.1021/bk-2019-1339.ch001.

273. Stephen Wampler, "LLNL-led team develops forensic method to identify people using human hair proteins," Lawrence Livermore National Laboratory website, llnl.gov, September 7, 2016.

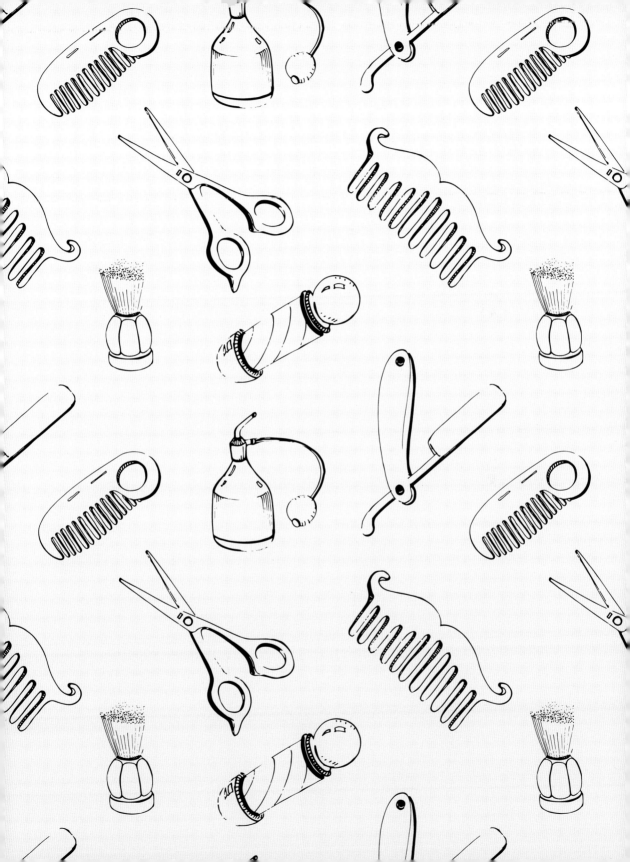

ACKNOWLEDGMENTS

*T*his section may come at the end of the book, positioned as part of the proverbial caboose, but without the kindness and skill of the special folks noted below, this train with its distinguished roster of hairy travelers across time would never have left the station.

My heartfelt thanks go out to the magnificent team at HarperCollins, including publisher Michael Aulisio, editorial director Marilyn Jansen, art director Jen Showalter Greenwalt, publicist MacKenzie Collier, senior editor Bonnie Honeycutt, and especially editors Kara Mannix and Kathleen Breaux, all of whose enthusiasm for this unusual book never waned; to artist Heather Gatley, for her wonderful illustrations; to long-time friends and manuscript readers Tom Panelas, Thad King, Robert Lewis, and Gregory McNamee; to my gracious endorsers Karen and Howard Baldwin, Jason Feifer, A.J. Jacobs, and Sudip Bose; to curators Lindsay Davenport of the Sagamore Hill National Historic Site, Kevin Moore of the Rutherford B. Hayes Presidential Library & Museums, and Robert McCracken Peck of the Academy of Natural Sciences of Drexel University; to reference librarian Paul Friday of the New Hampshire Historical Society, manager Sara Dobrowolski of the Franklin Pierce Homestead State Historic Site, and Marketing and Communications

Director Amy Raines of the George H.W. Bush Presidential Library and Museum; to historian and biographer Michael F. Holt of the University of Virginia, geneticist Christopher Tyler-Smith of Oxford University, and biochemist Martin Warren of the University of Kent; to renowned collector and authenticator John Reznikoff of University Archives; to former Navy psychiatrist Dr. Peter Harding, grandnephew of the president; to my wonderful sister, Tracey, as well as my children, who endured years of my rambling about this book before a single word ever inched toward pen and pad; and to hair stylist Jean Hood, my dear mother, and long-time friend and master stylist Janelle Renee of Elle Salon, for confirming for me, with stories from the front lines, that hair is seldom ever simply *hair*.

A deep debt of gratitude is owed to all.

IMAGE CREDITS

Department of the Army, Office of the Deputy Chief of Staff for Operations, US Army Audiovisual Center; Gerald Ford: David Hume Kennerly; Jimmy Carter: Department of Defense, Department of the Navy, Naval Photographic Center; Ronald Reagan: Michael Evans; George H. W. Bush: US Government; Bill Clinton: Bob McNeely, The White House; George W. Bush: Eric Draper; Barack Obama: Pete Souza; Donald Trump: Shealah Craighead; and Joe Biden: Adam Schultz

p. 2, Alexander Hesler, Library of Congress/public domain, via Wikimedia Commons

p. 3, unattributed, based on the depiction from a mechanical glass slide by T. M. McAllister of New York, c1865-75, restored by Adam Cuerden/public domain via Wikimedia Commons

p. 6, *Harper's Weekly*/public domain, via Wikimedia Commons

p. 7, Walt Whitman Papers in the Charles E. Feinberg Collection/public domain, via Library of Congress

p. 9, Library of Congress/public domain, via Wikimedia Commons

p. 12, painted by Thomas Hicks, lithograph by Leopold Grozelier/public domain, via Library of Congress

p. 14, Alexander Gardner/public domain, via Wikimedia Commons

p.19, Byron H. Rollins, *The Washington Post*/public domain, via Wikimedia Commons

p. 23, Anton Hohenstein/public domain, via Library of Congress

p. 25, George Peter Alexander Healy, The White House Historical Association/public domain via Wikimedia Commons

p. 28, Popular Graphic Arts/public domain, via Wikimedia Commons

p. 30, photographer unknown/public domain, via Wikimedia Commons

p. 33, photographer unknown/public domain, via Wikimedia Commons

p. 34, Julius Ulke/public domain, via Wikimedia Commons

p. 35, David Clark Burnite/public domain, via Wikimedia Commons

p. 38, National Museum of Health and Medicine/public domain, via Wikimedia Commons

p. 42-43, Alonzo Chappel/public domain, via Wikimedia Commons

p. 47, Science History Images/Alamy Stock Photo

p. 48, C. M. Gilbert/public domain, via Wikimedia Commons

p. 50, Gilbert Stuart/public domain, via Wikimedia Commons

p. 53, courtesy of Clara Barkley Dorr House museum

p. 54, John Michael Wright/public domain, via Wikimedia Commons

p. 58, Edward Anthony/public domain, via Wikimedia Commons

p. 60, top: courtesy of the Rutherford B. Hayes Presidential Library & Museums, Fremont, Ohio; bottom: courtesy of Sagamore Hill National Historic Site, National Park Service, Oyster Bay, New York

p. 63, Popular Graphic Arts, Library of Congress/public domain, via Wikimedia Commons

p. 64, unknown author, Missouri History Museum/public domain, via Wikimedia Commons

p. 67, courtesy of Peter A. Browne

p. 69, unknown author/public domain, via Wikimedia Commons

p. 72, Ralph Eleaser Whiteside Earl/public domain, via Wikimedia Commons

p. 74, Cecil W. Stoughton/public domain, via Wikimedia Commons

p. 76, Cecil W. Stoughton/public domain, via Wikimedia Commons

p. 78, USCapitol/public domain, via Wikimedia Commons

p. 79, Cecil W. Stoughton/public domain, via Wikimedia Commons

p. 86, michelangeloop/Shutterstock

p. 91, David Martin/public domain, via Wikimedia Commons

p. 93, Joseph-Syffred Duplessis, National Portrait Gallery/public domain, via Wikimedia Commons

p. 94, Chéri Hérouard/public domain, via Wikimedia Commons

p. 98, Frank Wolfe, LBJ Museum & Library/public domain, via Wikimedia Commons

p. 100, unknown author, Truman Library/public domain, via Wikimedia Commons

p. 101, National Archives and Records Administration, Office of Presidential Libraries, Harry S. Truman Library/public domain, via Wikimedia Commons

p. 103, Harris & Ewing, Library of Congress/public domain, via Wikimedia Commons

p. 104, unknown author, taken in St. Louis/public domain, via Wikimedia Commons

p. 106, Mathew Benjamin Brady/public domain, via Wikimedia Commons

p. 107, Cornell University Library/public domain, via Wikimedia Commons

p. 109, Harris & Ewing/public domain, via Wikimedia Commons

p. 110, National Photo Company Collection, Library of Congress/public domain, via Wikimedia Commons

p. 112, National Photo Company Collection/public domain, via Wikimedia Commons

p. 118, Jacques Lowe, Dell Publishing/public domain, via Wikimedia Commons

p. 120, Cecil Stoughton, National Archives and Records Administration/public domain, via Wikimedia Commons

p. 123, Walt Cisco, *Dallas Morning News*/public domain, via Wikimedia Commons

p. 124, Abbie Rowe, National Park Service/public domain, via Wikimedia Commons

p. 126, Associated Press/public domain, via Wikimedia Commons

p. 130, courtesy of Oliver Pappas

p. 131, Cecil W. Stoughton/public domain, via Wikimedia Commons

p. 132, Abbie Rowe, White House Photographs, John F. Kennedy Presidential Library and Museum, Boston/public domain, via Wikimedia Commons

p. 134, Aaron Shikler, White House Historical Association/public domain, via Wikimedia Commons

p. 137, Robert Knudsen, JFK Library/public domain, via Wikimedia Commons

p. 141, Mathew Benjamin Brady, Library of Congress/public domain, via Wikimedia Commons

p. 143, unknown author/public domain, via Wikimedia Commons

p. 145, George Peter Alexander Healy, National Portrait Gallery/public domain, via Wikimedia Commons

p. 147, Mathew Benjamin Brady/public domain, via Wikimedia Commons

p. 149, Presidential $1 Coin image from the United States Mint

p. 150, George Peter Alexander Healy, The White House Historical Association/public domain, via Wikimedia Commons

p. 152, Louise Altson, courtesy of the George H. W. Bush Presidential Library and Museum

p. 153, unknown author, George H.W. Bush Presidential Library and Museum/public domain, via Wikimedia Commons

p. 155, unknown author/public domain, via Wikimedia Commons

p. 159, Lauren Gerson/public domain, via Wikimedia Commons

p. 161, mark reinstein/Shutterstock

p. 162, Records of the White House Photo Office (George W. Bush Administration)/public domain, via Wikimedia Commons

p. 168, Jacques-Louis David/public domain, via Wikimedia Commons

p. 172, Clinton White House/public domain, via Wikimedia Commons

p. 180, Valentine Green, Gift of the Estate of John Ellerton Lodge/public domain, via Wikimedia Commons

p. 184, Harris & Ewing/public domain, via Wikimedia Commons

p. 188, Joseph Henry Bush, Gift of Mrs. Betty Taylor Dandridge, White House Historical Association/public domain, via Wikimedia Commons

p. 193, Nathaniel Currier/public domain, via National Portrait Gallery, Smithsonian Institution

p. 197, Allan Ramsay/public domain, via Wikimedia Commons

p. 199, Thomas Gainsborough and workshop, Staatliches Museum Schwerin/public domain, via Wikimedia Commons

p. 200, Wellcome Images/public domain, via Wikimedia Commons

p. 205, Tonhom1009/Shutterstock

ABOUT THE AUTHOR

Theodore Pappas has served as the Executive Editor of Encyclopaedia Britannica for more than twenty-five years. His writings have been published and discussed in numerous publications, including the *New York Times*, the *Los Angeles Times*, the *Chicago Tribune*, the *Wall Street Journal*, the *Spectator*, *The American Scholar*, the *New Yorker*, *Vanity Fair*, and *History Magazine*. He has appeared multiple times on the NBC show *TODAY*, as well as on *CBS Evening News*, *CBS News Sunday Morning*, CNN, Fox News radio and television, NPR's *All Things Considered*, and BBC Radio. He has written several books, the last one being *True Grit: Classic Tales of Perseverance*.